METAPHYSICAL DIVINE WISDOM
on Soul Consciousness and Purpose

A Practical Motivational Guide to Spirituality Series

Kevin Hunter

Warrior of Light Press

Copyright © 2019 Kevin Hunter
Cover copyright © 2019 by Warrior of Light Press

Published and distributed in the United States by Warrior of Light Press, which supports the right to free expression and the value of copyright. The purpose of copyright is to encourage writers and artists to produce creative works that enrich our culture.

All rights reserved. No part of this book and publication may be used or reproduced by any means including but not limited to digital, electronic, graphic, mechanical, photocopying, recording, taping or otherwise; nor may it be stored in a retrieval system, transmitted, or otherwise be copied for public or private use – other than for "fair use" as brief quotations embodied in articles and reviews - without the written permission of the copyright owner, publisher or author. Social media posts please credit the author. The scanning, uploading, and distribution of any contents in this book without permission is a theft of the author's intellectual property.

The author of this book does not dispense medical advice or prescribe the use of any technique as a form of treatment for physical, emotional, or medical problems without the advice of a physician, either directly or indirectly. The intent of the author is only to offer information of a general nature to help you in your quest for emotional and spiritual well-being. In the event, you use any of the information in this book for yourself, which is your constitutional right, the author and the publisher assume no responsibility for your actions.

Warrior of Light Press
www.kevin-hunter.com

First Edition: July 2019
Printed in the United States of America

All rights reserved. Copyright © 2019
ISBN-13: 978-1733196215

3. Mind and Body. 2. Spirituality. 1. Title

DEDICATION

For you on your soul's spiritual journey.

METAPHYSICAL DIVINE WISDOM
BOOK SERIES

On Psychic Spirit Team Heaven Communication
On Soul Consciousness and Purpose
On Increasing Prayer with Faith for an Abundant Life
On Balancing the Mind, Body, and Soul
On Manifesting Fearless Assertive Confidence
On Universal, Physical, Spiritual and Soul Love

♥

Contents

Chapter 1 — 1
Opening the Pathway to Divinity

Chapter 2 — 12
Knowing When Your Soul Is Transforming and Evolving

Chapter 3 — 26
Awakening Your Creative Consciousness

Chapter 4 — 41
Soul Contracts

Chapter 5 — 54
Life Purposes

Chapter 6 — 72
Healing and Transformation

Chapter 7 — 89
Soul Groups and Earth Angels

Chapter 8 — 103
The Earthly Birth

Chapter 9 — 112
The Soul and the Spirit

Chapter 10 — 126
The Higher Self

Chapter 11 ———————————————— 135
Soul Growth Through Grief

Chapter 12 ———————————————— 145
Soul Growth Through Health Issues

Chapter 13 ———————————————— 152
Soul Growth Through Relationships

Chapter 14 ———————————————— 159
Twin Flame Soul Mission and Purpose

Chapter 15 ———————————————— 171
Soul Growth Through Work and Career

Chapter 16 ———————————————— 178
Soul Growth Through Superficiality

Chapter 17 ———————————————— 186
Soul Growth Through Emotional Healing

Chapter 18 ———————————————— 196
The Human Influences on the Soul Consciousness

Chapter 19 ———————————————— 201
Spirit Guides and Guardian Angels

Chapter 20 ———————————————— 214
The Shift in Global Consciousness

AUTHOR NOTE

The *Metaphysical Divine Wisdom* books are a series of spiritually based books that focus on different areas of one's life. Like many of my spiritual related metaphysical books, this one is also infused with practical messages and spirit guidance that my Spirit team has taught and shared with me revolving around many different topics. The main goal is to fine-tune your body, mind, and soul. Like all souls, you are a Divine communicator capable of receiving messages and guidance from Heaven.

My personal Spirit team council make up God and the Holy Spirit, as well as a team of guides, angels, and sometimes Archangels and Saints. I am merely the liaison or messenger in delivering and interpreting the intentions of what they wish to communicate. My team comprises some hard truth telling Wise Ones from the Other Side, including Saint Nathaniel, who can be brutal in his direct forcefulness. He cuts right to the heart of humanity without apology. I have learned quite a bit from him while adopting his ideology, which is Heaven's philosophy. I wouldn't preach Divine Guidance that God doesn't whisper into my Clairaudient ear first.

If I use the word "He" when pertaining to God, this does not mean that I am advocating that he is a male. Simply replace the word, "He" with one you are comfortable using to identify God for you to be. If the word, "God" makes you uncomfortable, then substitute it with one you're more accustomed with like Universe, Spirit, Energy, the Light, or any other comparable word. This goes for any gender I use as examples. When I say, "spirit team", I am referring to a team of 'Guides and Angels'.

One of the purposes of my work is to empower, enlighten, as well as entertain. It's also to help you improve yourself, your soul, your life and humanity by default. If anything, I am preaching to myself, because God knows that I can use a refresher course occasionally. It does not matter if you are a beginner or well versed in the subject matter. There may be something that reminds you of something you already know or something that you were unaware of. We all have much to share with one another, as we are all one in the end.

~ Kevin Hunter

METAPHYSICAL DIVINE WISDOM
ON SOUL CONSCIOUSNESS AND PURPOSE

CHAPTER ONE

*Opening the Pathway
to Divinity*

Over the course of my life and in my spiritual teachings, I've conveyed wisdom that entails simple understood ways of improving your well-being, which instantaneously raises your soul's consciousness. Sometimes I might say something in conversation in a manner where it could be digestible to the recipient, but I cannot control if they ignore that or if it flies over them. I'm not going to hammer it into someone's psyche. I might do that in our books with the goal of cementing that concept into the consciousness, but not necessarily in random conversation.

One of the reasons my team and I talk and teach about this work is because I know that the level of the soul's consciousness upon death is the level that soul will gravitate towards back home in the Spirit world. If a soul like Mother Teresa is vibrating at a higher frequency such as where love, joy and peace reside, then that soul will gravitate towards a higher frequency of consciousness in Heaven. That soul will be pulled in the direction of those on a similar frequency. If the soul is vibrating on a lower level such as those that enact violence and hatred of any kind such as in the form of physical, emotional, including the nature of ones feelings and in words online, such as a simple social media post or comment, then that soul will be pulled in the direction of that energy upon death. It doesn't matter what platform that person is choosing to use, because the energy is attached to and traveling with that soul wherever it goes and whatever it inhabits including in a human being. This is the overall energy of your spirit's soul you are choosing to radiate at. When you vibrate on a higher frequency, then the spaces you inhabit in the Spirit world will be in that comparable frequency.

To describe it in a more practical way, the higher frequency vibrating soul would move into the areas where there are magnificent palaces amongst a vibrant colored paradise. Whereas the lower frequency vibrating soul would move towards an area where there are no actual homes, but a pile of wood to figure out how to put the impossible together yourself amongst a dry humid barren land filled with yellows, greys, and muddy browns.

This means that someone rich and famous on Earth with gorgeous palace like mansions in various places might be a toxic negative person, while someone poor in this life that struggles living check to check is a positive person. The positive person struggling in this life is pulled into the mansion like paradise on the Other Side, while the rich and famous person on Earth with the nasty attitude that treats people unkindly ends up being pulled into that barren land in the spirit world. This is just a quick and easy way to make the point, because it is much more layered than this.

One might say they don't believe in any of that the way some don't believe in a Hell, but why take that chance? Why not improve yourself if just for the sake of being a better person rather than for the sake of achieving that pot of gold.

Incidentally, what was described is like the concept that extreme religious people might believe that if you're a good Christian on Earth, then you will inherit the riches in Heaven, while the rest will go to Hell. It's a bit more complex than that, but the similarities with some of the teachings are obvious.

There are some souls unable to complete the dream like journey that ends when you puncture through the spirit plane and wind up being pulled into a left door or back gate where the energy vibrates on a lower level, then they'll wrap back around into another incarnation on Earth. This incarnation is one with additional lessons to endure in hopes that the soul will evolve upwards at least one notch than the previous lifetime. Otherwise the incarnations can go on indefinitely until the soul begins to show signs of evolving, which can mean positively changing all aspects of yourself.

Your Vibration and Consciousness

When there is talk of vibration, frequencies, energy, and a soul's consciousness, then this can fly right over the average person's head unless it's explained in simplified terms. A good deal of what is taught about the consciousness can come out convoluted. This makes it challenging to understand what is being explained. One of the goals of my guides working through me is the betterment of humanity. The advancement of Earthly civilization starts with you. It starts with one individual doing the soul growth work. It's a gradual often arduous process as one person evolves over time, which is simultaneously shifting their energy and consciousness. A positive shift in energy and consciousness in one person has a beneficial effect on those around them even if those around them are unaware they are in the presence of an evolving soul. The phrase to *lead by example* is to present your souls best self. This will rub off on those around you regardless if you think it's having a positive effect or not. It can shift one other person in the vicinity that begins to change themselves as a result of that. When they change, then this is passed on and so forth. This is one of the reasons why we're seeing more people partaking in some form of spiritual interests. Others are hearing about it through someone around them and this is triggering something remarkable within them.

Your consciousness needs to be awakened enough to allow you to see profound spiritual truths. No one can awaken your consciousness except you. It is the individual soul's job to do the work, research, study, and experience in order to strengthen your soul essence. This means not following the masses, but breaking away from the collective to find your personal soul path.

You are made up of energy the same way everything is made up of energy. How you direct that energy will dictate the essence of what will come back to you. If your feelings and thoughts are negative, then what is soon brought into your life is what matches that vibration. If your thoughts and feelings are positive, then this is the energy that is eventually brought into your life. There is no set time frame on how quick or slow something of equal or greater value to the energy matched with your feelings and thoughts is brought into your life.

A raised vibration coupled with life experiences helps in awakening your consciousness. When your consciousness is awakened, then you view Earthly life with a broader perception. Suddenly Earthly life in general appears trivial and superficial. You may start to feel permanently disconnected from it, isolated, and set apart from the norm. While this might cause you to stumble into a depression, understand that these are clues that your soul consciousness is expanding into something greater that awaits. A raised soul consciousness gives you a wider psychic perception that allows room for stronger cognitive input. This is the area where divinely guided information from above falls into and is planted.

Your vibration is made up of undetectable cells to the human eye, but visible to the spiritual eye. It is an invisible energy field that exists within the DNA of your soul, aura, and physical body. These cells fluctuate and change colors depending on your mood, your thought processes, your actions, who you surround yourself with, as well as what you ingest into your body. You are in control of this vibration energy field able to oversee and dictate how well you would like it to function through your life choices.

It's the same way you control other parts of your life such as the car you drive, to the house or apartment you live in, and so on. When you maintain your car, then you ensure it runs smoothly with routine check-ups, oil changes, checking the tire pressure, etc. This is similar to you taking care of your physical health as best as possible from getting regular check-ups, to watching the diet you consume, exercising regularly, to your overall daily state of mind. Taking care of your physical body affects your spiritual body. It's watching your thoughts and feelings to ensure they are on the positive side. All of this affects how bright or dim the energy field of your vibration radiates.

A High and Low Vibrational State

Your vibration can drop when you fall into a challenging negative state, which will happen on occasion. You get caught up in the routine and day-to-day practicalities of life and experiences that it leaves no room to check up on you, and how you're doing, and what your soul needs. The soul craves nourishment and the ego will at times interfere prompting you to reach for toxic substances to temporarily feed it, but which ultimately drain you leaving you wanting more.

When your vibration is low, you feel and experience negative feelings such as anger, depression, stress, irritability, and so on. When your vibration is high, you feel euphoric feelings of joy, love, peace, and contentment.

While in a higher vibration state, you'll find that what you desire moves into your vicinity quicker than if your well-being state was on the negative side. Your psychic intuitive awareness then grows allowing the heavenly spirit answers, messages, and guidance to come into your consciousness and through your psychic clair channels on a clearer level. The messages and guidance you receive is what helps you make sounder choices in your life.

A vibration in spiritual concepts is your overall emotional well-being and energetic state. Feelings such as depression, anger, and guilt lower your vibration, but if you're feeling joyful, in love, and centered, then your vibration begins to rise. The lowest vibrational state includes feelings of anger, stress, or depression. Watch out if you're experiencing a combination of all three at once.

The highest vibrational states are feelings of peace, joy, and love. It isn't a surprise that those traits are synonymous with the Christmas holiday season as a reminder to not forget your natural state of being. Experiencing all three of those states at the same time makes you a high vibrational powerhouse! Love is the highest vibrational state possible, so always revert to raising your emotional state to that of love.

You are born in a perfect state of high vibrational energy. Somewhere along the way rough tumultuous Earthly life circumstances shake your faith while knocking your vibration down in the process. When you're conscious of when this happens, then you can quickly re-align your vibration. I understand how hard that can be for those that live tougher stress filled lives. No one is exempt from Earthly life challenges, including the rich and famous. Even they are faced with their own challenges that might be similar or dissimilar to yours on a personal level outside of having financial riches. It's tough for some people to feel sympathy for someone that is financially well off, but no one is above or below anyone else in spiritual truth. No one gets a free pass from Earthly life challenges. Some of those challenges are ego self-induced, while others are spiritual lessons to help you grow and evolve.

Be mindful of your well-being state whenever possible, because a low vibration alters the energetic field around you. This blocks both divine guidance and positive circumstances from entering your vicinity. It tampers with your life on a spiritual and physical level. Being in a perpetual negative mood state can have health related consequences. When you have a high vibration, then positive experiences flow into your life. Your psychic antennae with the Other Side is also sharper where you're able to pick up on the messages and guidance coming in swiftly than if you were in a low vibration state.

Seeking the Path Towards Enlightenment

The lifelong battle with demons in my personal life is always matched with those from beyond the veil consistently pointing me towards the Light. When touched by the power, it is unconditional love experienced that no words can describe. The soul is overwhelmed in that radiance when enveloped in its arms. The answer to the question of the meaning of life is always the same. The answer is LOVE.

The more enlightened you become, and the more you raise your consciousness, then the better off you'll be. This doesn't mean that you'll be stress free, but you'll certainly experience less stress while being able to efficiently navigate through the treacherous waters of the practical world easier than if you did not have that raised consciousness.

Imagine if every human soul found the gift of love within them. No one would need to be here since that would be Utopia. When you find the space of love and learn to keep it there and revert to it when possible, then the closer you are to creating Heaven on Earth. It's a beautiful thing when one soul awakens another in a positive way just by being in their presence.

The rays of God's Light activate the soul propelling you into a Utopian paradise and beyond. The ultimate Nirvana is surpassing that perfection through methods a limited consciousness could ever dream possible. This is the exceptional glory your soul was born into before the dense turbulence of Earthy life enveloped and suffocated you.

Deep down every soul longs to re-attain and achieve that blissful excellence that gives the impression of unabashed joy and serenity. It is a condition where unwavering love and harmony surround you in a protected cushion. Transcending beyond the dull insensible frustrated Earthy life and into the natural condition the soul once habited is a goal that delights. It reminds the soul of where it came from. You runaway and travel around the globe searching for a sign of this utopia, only to be consistently left with disappointment. This is because utopia begins and ends inside the spark that burns within your soul like a pilot light.

Examine the negative emotions that initially impede your soul's movement. Start within and visualize this pilot light being ignited to the degree conceivable of generating a wildfire that expands in an explosion purging and clearing away all the darkness the ego consistently loses itself in.

The experiences you have in life both the practical and spiritual all play a part at shaping, molding, and evolving your soul's consciousness. In the coming chapters, we'll look at some of these areas.

CHAPTER TWO

Knowing When Your Soul Is Transforming and Evolving

There are some immediate signs that indicate if you or someone you know has incarnated from the Other Side with a bigger purpose. For one, you will know without a doubt what that mission is. You will already know that one of your life purposes is geared towards the betterment of humanity and the planet on some level. There is no, "I have no idea what my purpose is." Because if the purpose is a larger mission, then this is felt within the soul's DNA from as early as childhood. It may be that while in childhood, through the teenage years and into the beginnings of young adulthood that it might not be broadly clear what that mission is. The visions start to grow and expand within the soul's psychic senses early on. They include even tiny elements of that mission becoming largely evident to your consciousness. It is the person that by age fifteen that thinks, "I know there is a bigger reason I'm here beyond this nonsense."

Those with larger missions and purposes also tend to be evident people as early as childhood. There is something different than the norm with the child. This means the child will face ostracism by the lesser evolved that are unable to penetrate challenging depths at that time on their soul's unfolding process. They might be regularly bullied or called derogatory names like weird, freak, unusual, etc. Unfortunately, that's just what the higher evolving souls must deal with in earlier age when you're thrown into the center of the population that tends to operate on a superficial minimal level. Before you incarnated into this Earthly life, you're already aware of the challenges you'll face with hostile threatened human beings. If you're an outcast with broad visions within you that are greater than the mundane, then there is a high percentage of a chance that you are here for a larger mission and life purpose.

This drive for this mission propels you to contribute positive changes in that arena through action even if it means you will have to stand alone. And often you will end up standing alone on the ledge. Leaders tend to be the ones that view circumstances from a differing point of view than the rest of the masses. This enlightening process on the way to evolving your soul consciousness may not come to you right away. It can take a great deal of time and personal soul growth work contributions on your behalf before it cracks open. It may not come to you until well into adulthood, on your deathbed, and sometimes not at all. There is no rush to enlightenment because soul work operates on a different frequency than the physical human life work. The more life experiences, challenges, and lessons you endure tend to help one achieve enlightenment.

A teenager punk rocking drug user covered in tattoos might make one believe they have no purpose, but don't be fooled by their choices or form of personal self-expression at first glance. Strip away the external costume one chooses to wear this lifetime to peer into the soul's truth. Eradicate the labels burdened upon oneself such as black, white, gay, straight, male, female, liberal, conservative, and so on. Labeling confines you to a box and gives the illusion you have an identity, but when you limit and restrict yourself with a label, then you risk losing your soul's uniqueness. One of the goals of the human ego is to box you in, repress, limit, impede, and hold you down. It throws you in the passenger seat with blinders on and drives you over dangerous roads with speed bumps and traffic spikes. In that space you're unable to penetrate through any surface intended to expose reality.

To one extent a label needs to be used to give someone a deeper understanding of something when they're unable to come to that conclusion through telepathy, but you are not the labels you use to describe yourself in the end. The intention of labels is to divide and create separation. It compartmentalizes others into divisions not aligned with any soul's true existence. You lose authentic identity with a label since branding gives the illusion of a special uniqueness. You don't need a label to be exceptional because everyone's light shines when stripped of the outdated labels that ultimately break down and suppress who your soul is in long-term truth.

Individuality is evident without the need to distract through exclusions and groupings. Classifying others and forcing them into boxes creates unhealthy competition to one up each other and prove your group is the exceptional one. Once you do that, then you've handed the steering wheel to the darkness of ego that lives to push you down. There is no synchronization when you are out of alignment of your most indisputable self.

Back home all souls live in harmony regardless of being distinctive from one another. It's not on their radar to point out differences because eccentricity is honored and encouraged. Whereas on Earth the dissimilarities are shunned or feared because it makes the darkness of ego uncomfortable preferring that everyone be a clone. Stand out without hiding behind limitations and imperfections. Who are you without any outdated fads and labels you use to describe yourself?

Some people show signs of being a light worker, warrior of light, or other elements of a divinely guided trade, even though they might not be aware of it yet. It's easy to tell who is or who has that something unique about them that you know they're going to be evolving quicker than others over the course of their life. They may currently seem to be operating on a superficial level, but there are clues behind that surface where they display signs of something deeper going on.

Someone might not show obvious signs of being from a heavenly realm. Perhaps they gossip endlessly, live on a superficial level, display the darkness of ego beyond comprehension, but if you pay attention and look closer, you'll be amazed at what you find. At some point they may say something that shows an immense depth that will eventually one day break out in a bigger way with spiritual maturity. It's that one thing in a sea of superficiality that makes someone stop to ponder. This soul dramatically changes over the years becoming a different person entirely in the eyes of those around them.

Many from a heavenly realm tend to be either highly sensitive or highly addicted – sometimes both! Those who are super sensitive may fall into an addiction to mask, numb, or cushion this sensitivity, but this uncontrollable sensitivity is their calling card, winning streak, and the gift that needs maximum protection. The sensitivity and addiction gene are a clue that you are being asked to rise above that as best as you can. This way you can manage your life in a way that enables you to focus and put hard work into and towards the building of your life purpose. You have much to offer and don't want it to go to waste. It can take a lifetime of discipline to stay on your soul's path. You'll steer off course occasionally and have an off day, but when that happens drive right back up onto that express ramp and continue moving forward. Avoid beating yourself up when you veer off track on any given day. Allow yourself the day that you fell off the wagon knowing that you will get right back on path after you've worked through the emotions associated with falling off. Rinse and repeat this cycle until it becomes easier where you are deviating off course less and less. This doesn't mean you will never fall of course while you are moving through a stronger enlightening phase. You are going to have off days. It's just part of the human physical condition. Allow yourself to feel the pain or negative emotions associated with veering off course. It's all part of the soul's process. Whenever you are moving through that, then you are going through another soul transformation.

Surround yourself with positive people, friendships, hobbies, and endeavors that you know will prevent you from falling down a toxic path just by being in their presence. These are the kind of toxic paths that you are aware of that delay you from moving forward in doing what you need to do. Govern your life like a strict executive by being extra careful with who and what you allow in your environment, as well as what you put into your body.

None of that means you can't have any fun. Fun is all part of self-care pending you're not doing things that can harm any part of you whether spiritually or physically. Self-care is essential to your soul, so that you don't experience burnout. You need those regular days in between your passion and life purpose work where you devote to self-care to do things that bring you pleasure and joy. This contributes to a brighter balance in your world. The more balance you incorporate, the more equalized and steadier your soul feels.

For some people the enlightening process may come well into adulthood when the soul experiences what is called *the shift*. This is when you come to the realization that you had been going through the motions of what you've been trained to do by society and other human souls, but then there is a specific period or moment in your life where this shifts significantly. Something traumatic may happen in your life or you'll experience a deep moment of clarity where your mind and consciousness expands and cracks open. Your perception is permanently altered where you view human life in a different way than you had before that moment. This shift and turning point alters the trajectory you were previously on. Many of the interests you had leading up to that date and the things you once felt connected to no longer interest you. It's as if the shift happened over night where you wake up one morning literally and metaphorically. This is where you come to realize much of what has currently been going on in your life is no longer of interest to you.

For example, this could be like the job you once loved is no longer attractive to you, or the long-term friendships you have suddenly feel like strangers you no longer can relate to. Some of the people you had been close to feel like foreigners whose values and views are either different than yours, or they seem severely limited and too superficial for you to tolerate anymore. Their interests and personality no longer mesh well with yours as they once did. You don't have hatred or negative emotions about them. You appreciate them as the angels do about all souls, but on a personal level you've outgrown them. You know you once agreed with them on important issues and had the same perception, but your soul expanded during its spiritual transformation and it grew beyond that. This isn't the kind of feeling that comes and goes, but a feeling that comes and never leaves you beyond that day of realization. It doesn't mean you have no love for them, but the new transformed you can no longer relate to them.

During my drug addicted days in my early twenties, I knew that I was no longer interested in that. I had a mission and purpose that I didn't want to be ruined by my adolescent rebelliousness. After I stopped the drugs, I was still going to the drug lord's homes to hang out with them. They were all partying, but I wasn't consuming anything. About a month in I thought, "What am I doing here? I can't relate to anybody here now that I'm sober."

You gradually dissolve those connections naturally like you're shedding the cocoon you had been living in. You release them with love remembering the blessings and lessons learned while with them. Some of them may remain in your life, while others will gradually dissipate away where you're seeing them less and less. You don't even necessarily have to do anything, as it's often a natural process where you are both growing more distant due to the wide discord.

Friendships that were once close have dissolved in this same way for others that have gone through similar spiritual transformations. It wasn't due to a problem that created a fight or a disagreement, but that you or they were peering out with new eyes. Your perception has been so radically altered that your values and whole being presented seem like another person entirely that you may not even recognize yourself anymore. The gears have shifted, and you head down a different path that is no longer in line with those you were once close to. Others may naturally transition with you down this new path and begin showing signs of evolving as well. This brings on a deeper connection than you had before.

This isn't a temporary shift, but a permanent one where you begin the process of making both major and minor changes to your life over the months and years to come. This is another sign that you are evolving. It's also realizing that the way things are on the planet is not normal just because humankind at that time in history says so. From an early age you're automatically suspicious of the current way that human life is and its structures, but by adulthood you've broken off that piece. You have a higher view of the triviality that others find themselves trapped in.

Technology has taught, trained, amplified, and exaggerated aggressive behavior without considering the consequences. In 2005, I saw the coming of an uprising of a major ongoing culture war around the world that would take place in bigger ways than could be comprehended at the time. It was a culture war that could ultimately destroy the planet over the coming centuries if changes were not made individually. In order to change globally you must change individually one person at a time. You must ask yourself if you're part of the problem or are you going to be one of the solutions contributing your part.

God sends His best to Earth that can viciously stay centered amidst the lower energy fueling system instigated by the darkness of ego. He knows only His best is more than capable of climbing back up if they get knocked down. Earth is a battlefield and you are His soldier hired to do His will. Falling into where everyone else is going does not lead to salvation. It leads to an avalanche of misery. Energy grows and expands regardless if it is Light or Dark energy. If it's miserable Dark energy, then it can and will eat and consume the soul. It's a pain that never lightens up.

When you're moving through a spiritual transformation, then you may start to feel more alien and detached from the masses entirely. You find you don't agree with anything that's going on in the media on either side or amongst your peers. You see everyone functioning in a limited way, which further alienates and isolates you from the nonsense. You are unable to relate or connect to anyone closely, with the exception being the trusted ones around you. This can create an isolating lonely feeling, but evolving souls are usually comfortable alone. They don't typically crave attention and praise from anyone. Your sensitivities become more enhanced because your psychic senses are growing more enriched. The two are interconnected which can lead you to be susceptible to absorbing in all that negative energy on the planet, which lowers your vibration and sucks the life force right out of you.

It's not God's job to absolve anyone from their sins nor give anyone a free pass to behave badly. It's up to the individual soul to learn from their mistakes in order to grow and evolve their soul's consciousness. All souls are evolving on Earth with whatever endeavor they undertake on their own time and in their own way that's most comfortable for that soul. There are also a great number of souls who never change, evolve, or shift at all throughout one lifetime. They will undergo numerous lifetimes to gain knowledge with the intent that it will eventually awaken and broaden their consciousness beyond the physical limitations they're trained to focus on.

One of the many goals of a soul in a human body is to grow, expand, evolve, and eventually transform. Some never reach those levels in their first life run, while other more advancing souls are transforming rapidly and repeatedly accelerating beyond comprehension than the norm for a human being. Transforming is not an easy process, because of the pain involved. The pain can be so great that having suicidal or despairing thoughts isn't unusual. You feel like the pain is too much, but then you take a step back and realize your souls' purpose is greater than the temporary pain you're feeling in that moment.

A transformation is full of all kinds of feelings. I've been through so many of them that I'd love to say I'm used to it. Some of them are harder than others. The more challenging ones I can sense when it's coming up on the horizon. It could be building up the months or even a year prior as I start to psychically sense that I'm heading for that transformation. Once the transformation has hit, then it can take months to get through as there's a metaphorical shedding of the skin kind of like a caterpillar transforming into a butterfly. The caterpillar goes into a cocoon where it appears motionless. This can be aligned with you feeling as if nothing is moving in your life no matter how hard you try. You feel this long stagnancy going on when in actuality you are moving through the caterpillar's cocoon stage. It requires a great deal of faith and patience to understand things are brewing underneath even when it doesn't feel like that. There is no time limit before you break out of the cocoon and into a butterfly.

I've had major things around me being wiped away to make room for the next chapter. I could psychically see it coming, then this would cause a feeling of dread over it. Sometimes as I'm seeing it, I'm thinking, "Oh no I don't want to transform again. It's too much."

Deep down I still know that the more you transform, then the more you evolve your soul. On the flipside, I could never stay the same since that would drive me crazy. When things start getting too rigid or stale, I know another spiritual soul transformation is coming again.

During that transformation process everything comes into question. Relationships, jobs, social roles, goals, etc. New experiences personal and professional come in as the old is dissolving. When I've had those kinds of major transformations, I could feel the weight of the previous chapter of my life tightening up and strangling me. The Archangel Nathaniel specifically comes in to extract all the old in your life and rip it out whether you want it to or not. It's so abrupt that it can feel like the end of the world or that it's as if it's one bad thing happening after another. It's only when you take a step back to have the higher perspective that the angels have, then you understand that something greater is in motion and at play for you. This is where you can now say, "God has a plan right now and I'm going to trust Him on it."

The larger transformations I've had were so lengthy and difficult that I knew it was the end of a chapter. This psychic foresight was giving me panic attacks before it arrived because I knew it was coming. Even though I also knew it was a good thing in the end. It doesn't mean the intensity of the visions weren't pounding on my psychic system. You are constantly building your soul the way cities were built from nothing. Our souls are like the water that flows like the Ocean tides. It was made to continuously move and transform and evolve.

When you've had a great deal of intense life being experienced in a short amount of time, then the positive aspects to that are the soul strengthening traits coming out of those experiences and lessons. It's going to direct you into your next chapter, which will be grand and beyond expectations. If you've made it this far through all the challenges, the distress, pain, excitement, then celebrate that! Celebrate the life you have. Break open a bottle and rejoice in that soul win. When you transform and evolve it never means you have fully evolved. If you peak, then you lose life force again. Therefore, the soul's goal is to continuously transform and evolve. The gift that comes with your final challenge is your next challenge.

CHAPTER THREE

*Awakening Your
Creative Consciousness*

Awakening your creative spirit within has many benefits that are connected to simultaneously expanding your soul's consciousness. When you dive into creative hobbies or pursuits, then you are utilizing and working out parts of your psychic intuition that may have been dormant. The benefits to breathing life into your psychic senses is that this helps you pick up on the Divine guidance and messages that your Spirit team can be urging you to do. Their role is to guide you throughout your life in steps, but this doesn't do you any good if you're unable to psychically pick up on what they're giving you. This is one of the various reasons as to why paying attention to that creative part of you can help in expanding those psychic gifts that already reside within your soul's DNA.

Nurturing your creative spirit assists in tapping into parts of your soul consciousness that awaken it. Your creative spirit is present when you experience positive energy flowing through you. This energy is ignited when you make a direct connection with God. This vibration state is where you have access to the true you, which is your higher self the soul part of you in its glorious perfection before it was born into an Earthly life.

Your higher self can take hold of the reigns of your life when you work to strip, reduce, or dissolve any negative tampering influenced by the domination of your physical surroundings. Make a connection with something greater than yourself by allowing that Divine energy Light to permeate your soul and cleanse it of toxic debris. This will assist in the process of awakening your creative spirit from slumber.

Your creative spirit is more than being artistic and getting involved in creativity pursuits, although this is a good part of it. When your creative spirit is activated by a high vibrational state of being, then this is the space you create and intuit from. You can apply this to your dealings in life, your creative and artistic endeavors, and to having a greater communication line with your Spirit team on the Other Side. Your creative spirit helps brings your soul into a high vibrational state of being because coming from a place of creativity raises your vibration. This is the zone where you create and manifest your visions at higher levels, while concurrently moving you into the joy of your life. It includes thinking like a kid, unleashing your inner artist, and coming to the realization of your souls potential. When you claim your celestial power with the assistance of your Spirit team of heavenly helpers by your side, then this assists in capitalizing the true divine power within you. This is part of what it means to have access to Divine assistance and how that plays a part in arousing the muse within you in order to bring your state of mind into a happier vibrational state.

Your Spirit Team

When your soul enters its Earthly life in a human body, you are not born alone. One Spirit Guide and one Guardian Angel accompany you. They are your "Spirit Team" that will remain by your side from birth until you cross back over in human death. The goal they have with you is to ensure you stay on the right path that benefits your higher self. When you pay attention to their nudges, guidance, and messages, then the happier and more content your life is. When you do not follow their guidance, or take notice of when they are helping, then your life becomes chaotic, stressful, or anxiety ridden. If you are someone that works with Heaven, angels, God, archangels, saints, or any higher being in the spirit world regularly, then you will attract more guides and spirit Light energy sources into your vicinity that desire to help you.

Some of them enter your aura to bask in your own soul's light, which is like a warm sun on a gorgeous Spring day.

One of God's gifts to human souls are also the Archangels and Angels, which are His hands and arms assisting and guiding you to raise your vibration so that you will better be able to hear God. When you connect or communicate with an Archangel or Angel, then you are connecting with God. You are not praying to the Angels, since they are a part of Him. When your vibration is low, then your connection to God is cut off. The angels and archangels help you to reach Him. Being connected to the Light is what contributes to your souls evolving process.

There are additional heavenly helpers that may come into your life during key transformation and transitional periods in your life when it's most needed. This can be from a project you're working on that will be of benefit to you or others. They will also be present to ease your mind and heart during times of grieving and sadness. The grieving can be over the death of someone close to you, from a broken love relationship, or during periods of depression. Once the additional guides or angels outside of your team have accomplished a quest with you, they leave to assist others, or they will go where they are guided to or needed. All in Heaven desire to serve because they either have no ego or little ego. When you use the dark side of your ego, then you do not care about others. When the ego part of a human being shows that it cares, then it could be masking an ulterior motive with the interest of personal gain.

You are born psychic and in tune to all that is beyond the physical world. This is the natural state of your soul. You are also born operating with high vibrational qualities such as love, joy, and peace. All of this begins to fade in varying degrees due to human tampering and distractions during adolescence and your developmental years. Your surroundings contain your caregivers, peers, the media you watch, and the community you reside in. All of this influences you on how to think, and what to follow, or what to believe in. This affects the rate as to how fast or slow your soul's consciousness will move through its many evolving processes.

The Larger Lights of Children and Animals

Children and animals have the highest ranges of psychic abilities than any other. Children haven't been fully tampered with and destroyed by jaded adults. When a child is scared or explains that they're seeing something no one else is, an adult automatically tells them, "Oh, it's just your imagination." There isn't a worse phrase to tell a child that is confiding in you about something that may be present that a cynical adult no longer understands. This phrase is what begins the process of erecting blocks to Divine communication in that child's life. In all fairness, it's not the adult's fault entirely. They are a product of the environment they were raised in. They we're trained to view things that are not understood by the ego to be a figment of one's imagination. Be open minded to what a child is telling you. They see, hear, feel, and know far more than adults give them credit for.

Animals remain as the spirit beings with the higher psychic ranges throughout the course of its life. It doesn't have the kinds of blocks that human souls create. An animal isn't concerned with paying rent or a mortgage. It's not concerned about finding work or stressing out over triviality and superficiality. If it's fed, has a place to sleep, and with an owner who loves it, then there are little blocks in its world if any at all.

Imagination is the source where your creative spirit is awakened. This space is the portal that leads to a stronger communication line with Heaven. The artists of the world and throughout history have greater access to the Divine because they have a good degree of sensitivity and imagination. They can walk through another's shoes without judgment no matter horrible that other person might be. Gifted actors excel at this as well. This open mindedness is one of the keys to having a crystal-clear connection line with your Spirit team.

It's not uncommon for those in childhood and teen years to have super strong connections with the Other Side, but it may be accompanied with the fear of wondering who is around them or why. Sometimes those who appear for them are Guides or Angels, and other times they are spirits who have not crossed over into the light and are unaware that they've gone. They're stuck in the transition between the Earth and spiritual plane. Spirits are attracted to the Light whether already on the Other Side or in this plane. Since children and animals tend to have larger lights around them than adults, then this makes them a magnet for spirits that have been stuck between this plane and the next. Children and animals have these larger lights because they haven't been stripped of this light due to blocks created in the physical world. Therefore, the spirit tends to gravitate and surround them. They're attracted to the light and the life force of the human soul. This also means they're attracted to adults that have a stronger psychic sense and a larger light around them. It's like being attracted to anything where you want to get close to it and feel it. Some young people are so fearful of it that overtime as they grow older the connection and light dims. As a result, they refuse to acknowledge it as an adult.

Breaking Away from the Norm

Those that preach about God and Heaven in a negative, hate filled, prejudicial way with vengeful angry words that attack other people are not communicating with God, since there are no negative words uttered from Him. Those words come from the Darkness or the Devil as some call it which influences the human ego. The darkness of ego separates the good that exists in humanity and instead creates labels to ensure all souls are estranged from one another. All human souls are siblings of each other, since they were birthed out of the one source, but their light begins vibrating at different frequencies depending on its influences.

Others have been turning their backs on any mention of the word God because of the stigma that misguided souls have preached. They insist that God disapproves of you, which could not be further from the truth. His immense love for you is unconditional. He only expects that you put in effort to be a better more compassionate person. Evolve your soul in order to move onto brighter destinies. This isn't any different than what a good parent desires for their child.

The Earth plane is a place for all student souls, whether they are here for the first time since they sparked out of God, or if they are experiencing a repeat life in order to continue their soul's education so they can continue to expand and evolve. They cannot move on until individual soul lessons are learned, gained, and accepted. The student souls are called *Baby Souls*. They are more naïve and innocent, yet some of them are filled with hate and destruction because they have not mastered the ego. The ego became this way due to how they were raised in their environment. Hate and negativity are passed down into the human child. When you train your child early on to have love and compassion for all souls, then they will grow up this way.

The in-tune soul can sense a low vibration

within a baby soul that seems to be permanent, but, is temporary. The vibration is stuck vibrating at a lower level until the soul awakens its consciousness. This typically comes through with experience and knowledge gained while on Earth. It is breaking away from the masses to realize there is more at play than what is being fed by others. Until then it is unable to expand, but instead stays exactly where it is swimming around in hatred and negativity. Some of them are also cruel, insulting, or power hungry. They are driven to put others down whether through domination or by bullying. You likely have an image of who someone like this is unless you've been cut off from all media sources and people.

When you visit certain places around the world, you'll notice that those who live in that specific community are all mostly like one another. Things like they may follow the same religion or vote for the same political candidates. They have similar rituals, opinions, and belief systems, etc. There might be some minor differences, but for the most part they behave quite the same as one another. They are clones going along with everyone else in order to not rock the boat, to fit in, or be accepted.

There are those that reside in these communities that the majority considers to be the oddball, weird, or different. Those are the ones that the community considers to be unusual from the rest of them. They are unable to hide who their soul truly is. They will eventually reach a point of defying that if they hadn't from the beginning. They tend to be the ones destined for greater purposes.

Unable to suppress their true creative spirit, they're also usually the ones able to access spirit easily.

It takes great strength to see, feel, think, and do things differently than those around you. Think for yourself even if it defies what society or the community around you consider to be normal. Normalcy is a guideline that one's community insisted upon with one another, but it doesn't necessarily mean they're right. What is considered the norm is not always the case from the point of view of Spirit. It's just what the human community you are surrounded by trained you to believe.

The human mind has a great capacity for awesomeness, but the lower part of the human mind will follow anyone dangling a carrot in front of it. Your surroundings and the media tell you how to think, act, and who to lynch, or who to support. Human souls move like herds following someone they believe to be a good shepherd, or whoever their peers are raving about, or whatever fads happen to be in at that time in history. Easily influenced and swayed within their community instead of doing the hard work and research to find the highest truth.

The lone wolf that turns away from the crowd and walks in the other direction is usually a leader or guide in the making. They view things differently than the majority around them do. Often, they incarnated for a specific purpose that prompts others to view things in a broader way that eventually influences others to follow or learn from. History has shown that those that were ostracized, hated, or criticized tended to have the most positive beneficial impact in contributions towards the betterment of humanity. They might be that person who conveys compassion to all no matter what, even when the lynch mob around them is attacking or bullying someone else.

The surroundings you grow up around can wreak havoc on your soul's inner core-built system during your developmental years. This is carried on your soul's back indefinitely until it begins the laborious process of stripping away negative habits and values that were learned. This toxicity gives rise to the darker part of your ego or lower self. Your ego will do what it can to sabotage you. It can be greatly convincing that it's as if you've been taken over by the Devil himself.

The Darkness resides in one of the spirit planes that is in an interdimensional existence with this one working to poison and infect as many as possible, since it's so easy to do. It will bring out your lower self that views circumstances and others through a bleak, toxic, and often dangerous view. This is predominately evident in those that bully, harass, and call others derogatory names on their platform of choice. The darkness has infected that soul poisoning it with lies that cause harm and destruction. It helps no one around including the one dishing the harmful words, since it lowers that person's vibration as well. It's a waste of unnecessary energy that blocks good things from entering that person's life. Instead it invites in more negativity and ultimately creates the downfall and fate of that soul's consciousness.

Rise Up into Your Glorious Soul Power

Your inner light operates out of a high vibration. You have access to it since it never leaves you. When your vibration drops, then your ego and lower self rise simultaneously. This is followed by a weakening of your inner light to the level of a pilot light waiting to be re-ignited. When it is re-ignited, then the light begins to grow and fills up your soul like a wildfire that pushes your higher self back to the forefront of your life. The bigger the flame, then the more light it attracts in. When the light expands, then this contributes positively to your evolving process, which raises your consciousness giving you deeper psychic perception. This light is the doorway to God *(Spirit, Light, Essence, Power, All Knowing, the Creator, Energy, etc.)* It is where the helpful guidance and messages come in from spirit to help you along your path. It is what assists you in attracting in your desires pending that it is aligned with your higher self's goal. It is the part of you that is psychic and in tune.

Having confidence in you is having confidence in God. The best parts of you are what God is. He is not a man with a beard sitting high up on a throne looking for ways to judge you. The ego is what judges' others negatively. God is made up of energy that has the highest vibrational traits imaginable. He is made up of love, joy, peace, confidence, optimism, forgiveness, and grace. Because His vibration is so high to the point that it's not comprehensible, this makes it difficult for human souls to reach Him. You cannot reach him when exuding any measure of negative emotion.

Raise Your Consciousness

Negativity on any level can block you from achieving. Every soul is deserving of good on the planet, and every single person has something positive to offer. In higher spiritual truth, no one is more special than anyone else or below or above another, because all souls were made equally. Some souls have an easier time at evolving their consciousness than others. While other souls remain at one level throughout one Earthly lifetime.

In Heaven, all souls are considered one united. This is how it is supposed to be on Earth, even though the human ego convinces some people that they're either better or worse than another. It can be seen this way when you compare a giving Saint to a terrorist killer. In that comparison the differences are wide, but this is about both of those people's souls deep down at the core. When the soul is born into an Earthly life, then it is born with the highest God like qualities available and imaginable. It is only as the soul moves through its human journey do the experiences it endures shape and mold them to something else entirely.

The Godly traits the soul is born with are always inside them and forever accessible. The soul has to figure it out for itself and do the work to bring it back out again. As you're likely aware, not many accept that challenge and they end up suffering. Remembering your soul's true heritage makes you a powerful soul.

Every time you learn lessons that propel your soul forward spiritual growth is achieved. It is the knowledge gained through each experience that contributes to progress. This is regardless if the experience is challenging or positively enjoyable. It will still add to molding, shaping, and expanding your consciousness to greater heights. Sitting around in front of the television all day everyday accomplishing nothing of value will ensure your soul's growth remains in the same place. The exception to that is if someone is an invalid or battling a health issue. The health issue in this case is offering mental struggles and will power that strengthen and grow your soul. The opposite kind is if you plop on the sofa staring at trash television all day out of laziness.

You cannot watch reality television regularly or read gossip content daily and raise your conscious. This doesn't mean you have to avoid those things completely if you have interest in them, but typically a higher vibrating soul doesn't have much of an interest in those types of things. It's considered an unhealthy addiction due to the dumbed down content that enforces a stereotypical shallow existence, which is also having that same effect on your soul. This is about the offenders that spend their days absorbing this energy with no interest in anything else, rather than the occasional fun and playful curiosity you might have in a rare story.

Raising your consciousness is important because remaining stunted in terms of soul growth ensures that karma is built up and an Earthly life do over in a tougher circumstance is inevitable. God sees that the one life run was wasted and didn't work. Having to do it again in a tougher circumstance life situation has a greater chance of placing enough Earthly life challenges to help your soul be snapped into long term soul reality that there is something greater at play than the Earthly life mundane that human beings set up. This is the same as a Wise One task master Teacher in school that gives the students a harder test than the one before in order to challenge them. This isn't done in punishment, but to help them grow and expand their mind and consciousness so they may graduate into something grander than where they are now.

There isn't one main event that assists in your spiritual growth, but numerous mini events interwoven throughout your Earthly life. When you feel like it's one thing after another going on in your world, then look at that as being lessons you are enduring for a greater purpose as hard as that might feel at the time. Know that nothing stays the same and this challenge too shall pass. Major events will offer larger growth experiences, but the mini events are just as important if not more so. The side effect to the events is that it helps you make sounder decisions, which help you live a more prosperous and abundant life.

CHAPTER FOUR

Soul Contracts

Before you enter an Earthly life, your soul got together with a council of highly evolved heavenly leaders that work with you to put a soul contract together. The soul contract includes many of the main events that will happen in your life and the reasons for those events. The many soul mates you'll encounter will also be listed along with the estimated dates that they show up. Everything in the soul contract is a forecasted estimation, because you and those around you in the contract are also granted free will choice to do what you or they want to do. Paying attention to God and your Spirit team helps you fulfill your destinies and bullet points within this contract. You ask for their help when needed, you follow their guidance, and act when necessary.

When you ignore God and your Spirit team, then you are also ignoring some of the things that are in your souls' contract. They are trying to help you fulfill elements in your souls' contract. They will repeatedly put up the same signs in your path to get you to notice it in hopes you'll act on it. If you continue to ignore it, then that same sign will continue if it needs to. For some people the same sign never goes away. When they reach human senior age or their final years, they might conclude that there were things they were supposed to do, but they never did. Those things were in their souls' contract, but they ignored it and chose to set out to have a different life. One of the harder things to see is someone express regret at the end, instead of finding ways to accomplish, do, and see what they intended while here.

When they arrive back home in Heaven, one of the main things they do beyond reuniting with some of their loved ones is they want to get their hands on that soul contract. They will see all the things they were supposed to accomplish and what they failed to accomplish. They'll also recall instances in their Earthly life when they were clearly being shown to do something that is affiliated with this soul contract, but their human ego denied or ignored it. This is also due to the many blocks that were present preventing them from accurately picking up on that Divine guidance coming in from their Spirit team. God and your Spirit team are not pushing or urging you towards something for no reason. There is a purpose behind their guidance. The soul develops amnesia when it incarnates into a human body. Part of that is for their protection. If they knew exactly what was to take place, then they would never live life. They would sit around and wait for it to happen.

If the soul sits around waiting for the contracted events to take place, they would waste their time because the events would not happen due to their free will choice to sit and wait for it. The soul has many purposes it needs to set out to do while here. Each human soul is given just enough information from Spirit at the right time allowable on God's timing. Even the most psychic person on the planet won't be able to see everything. They can only see what God allows them to see at that moment, which can come through in psychic snippets and flashes. Sometimes enduring a severe crushing struggling phase is part of your soul's contract. There is an added benefit to your soul's growing consciousness.

What is also drawn out and included in this lengthy soul contract that can fill a gigantic book are the experiences you agree to endure in that Earthly lifetime. This includes your life purpose, goals, lessons, missions, and the challenges you will face. There are various bullet points listed that assist in the growth and evolvement of your soul. Also included in this contract are the soul mates and karmic connections you will meet along your journey. These relationships are intended to assist in expanding and growing your soul. They include family members, friendships, colleagues, acquaintances, and lovers. They make up the many soul mates you encounter in your life.

When the contract is drawn up in Heaven, also listed is that there will be different special guides or angels that will show up temporarily to help the soul with pivotal events, such as getting the right jobs, finding the right soul mate partners, and on up to greater quests that help humanity in a positive way. One is not always at the same job for a lifetime. They will endure many different jobs that they are gaining important qualities, skills, and traits from. They will then apply those additional gained qualities to their next chapter. The same goes for soul mate partners, which is also why many have many different soul mates sifting in and out of their lives. Those waiting for that one special soul mate are unaware they have more than one that will come in the form of friendships, family members, colleagues, acquaintances and in love relationships.

Look at every single job or people you've encountered throughout your life, whether good or bad, and examine all the positive benefits you gained that helped in your evolving growth process. The more you evolve your consciousness, then the easier it is to detect what you learned. If you're unable to see what you learned, then you will continuously encounter similar soul mate people and situations throughout your life that are teaching you the same lesson. This is in their soul's contract to be of added benefit to your soul. On a subconscious level, their soul knows what it is they will be bringing to your life, with you bringing something of benefit to them. All soul relationships are both a teaching and learning situation on both sides.

There is something you are intended to gain even through the meanest person you meet. What have you learned from those types of connections? You will be given similar soul mates from one another when a lesson isn't being learned hard enough. Eventually this cycle stops when you have the spiritual awakening and awareness that you are constantly attracting in the same types in. That's when you need to take a good hard look to discover why your soul is continuously pulled into the same repetitive circumstances. This is also a clue as to what your soul's many purposes are to accomplish in this life, since not all life purposes are a financially driven and lucrative career. The same way you have more than one soul mate, you also have more than one life purpose within one lifetime. All of this and much more are in this soul contract.

You are also set up with three separate departure times throughout your Earthly lifetime. If the first two points of Earthly departure are denied and decided against, then the third departure time is the Earthly death. It is the maximum allowable time you've agreed upon in living one Earthly life. You might even recall one or two previous moments where you almost died. These are not the same as near death experiences which are enacted to awaken the soul that needs to be awakened for a greater purpose.

Your soul contract is in a personal book devoted

to you that the Archangel Metatron keeps in the Hall of Records in Heaven that some call the Akashic Records. There are key circumstances that are listed to take place in it, but that doesn't mean every single one of those bullet points will happen. Things like free will choice can delay or negate it all together. For example, in the book it might state that you'll meet a love partner at age twenty-eight. It describes who that person is and other details about them as well as where and when you'll meet them. Due to free will choice and other unforeseen circumstances beyond your control or this other person's control, delays can push it out, then you find that you end up meeting this person at age thirty-six. The delays or free will choices pushed the circumstance further out, while in other cases delays and free will choices are so great that it pushes it out indefinitely. The path crossing with this person never happens or it comes so close, but you both miss it.

All human souls have the capacity to see, feel, know, and hear messages and guidance from beyond. Everyone is equally and unequivocally psychic for the purpose of being able to connect with their Spirit team. You're on a mission on Earth and they are guiding you with that mission. If you are not picking up on anything psychically, then that means you are experiencing a block. Blocks form easily in the physical Earthly life since the physical life is a challenging one. Human beings generate most of the problems that exist. If there were no human beings on the planet, then the planet's energy life force would evolve and re-grow itself on its own without the tampering destruction that people tend to wreak on it.

Endless data of information exists in this soul contract. This contract is more than a sheet of paper or the kind of contract you expect to receive for a job position. The duties listed in a human job contract are not far off from the nature of the soul contract, which lists an array of duties and purposes you're agreeing to work towards accomplishing for the benefit of your soul. One core difference between the soul contract and a regular job contract is that you cannot get fired for not performing your soul duties. Every soul contract is also large enough to fill numerous large books that house each soul's lifetimes on Earth, galaxies, and dimensions. Not only does the contract list your purposes and core events scheduled to take place, but everything you do or do not do in your entire soul's history is also recorded in this book. Everything you can ever imagine about you is in this contract.

Much of the challenges the soul endures are also listed in the soul's contract in the Hall of Records on the Other Side. This Hall of Records is no ordinary library. It contains all the answers to anything and everything that a soul could possibly want to know. Placing your hand on it allows the information to be filtered rapidly into your soul's consciousness like a computer uploading data.

One of the many agreements contained in the soul contract is a set up that lays out numerous paths that branch out into other numerous roads. It looks like the LIFE board game, but is a hundred times more complex.

If you miss one fork in the road and head down a different path it might reveal that you would take the longer route around before you reach your destination. What is interesting is that most of the roads lead to the same destination, with a percentage of souls heading in a completely different direction due to the free will choice action of the individual.

An event intended to take place may be soul contracted, but no spirit being can interfere with your free will choice. This is still your life to live it for you. Your Spirit team will do their best to gently guide you towards the direction you originally agreed upon, but your ego can override that and choose to do what it wants you to do. As a result, you end up being taken for a ride in another direction.

Some paths take the longer away around, while others might have more challenges listed on them. As mentioned, there are also the three exit points that indicate the main sections of your life where your soul may choose to exit this life and head back home. There are also agreements indicating the various soul mates you'll encounter along your life path. It also lists the purposes and intentions that you and each soul mate will have with one another. These include the numerous lessons you've both agreed to endure for the benefit of soul growth, which affects the evolving soul consciousness.

Because you have free will choice, this can negate and alter what is intended to take place. This contract may reveal a love soul mate showing up at a particular time. Due to free will choice on your part and/or this other person's part, it can alter and change both your paths pushing the connection further out or from happening at all.

One example is it can be something such as remaining with a current partner that was supposed to end awhile back, but didn't for various reasons. The next partner soul mate rarely shows up before the previous one is absolutely without a doubt complete. In some cases, the next soul mate partnership does show up, but you both fail to acknowledge one another or pay attention due to having one foot cemented in the previous connection refusing to give up and walk away. You know that previous connection was supposed to end a long time ago because it's usually bathed in toxic unstable issues. Your free will choice can convince you to stay longer than you should have for fear of what might happen or not happen.

Other times, the ego will put you through a denial phase where you believe without a doubt this person is the one, you're supposed to be with, but the other person is failing to see that. As a result, you cling to that person not realizing you had been deceived by the ego to drag it on longer than it was intended to. When it is the right person for you, there will be no resistance coming on either side. It will happen as natural as it would in a romantic comedy.

Sometimes the future soul mate love partner will show up while you're still in the connection that was supposed to end. You feel a strong gravitational pull towards that new person even though you might not romantically act on anything with them. Both teams of guides from your side and this other person's side are aware that the old connection is going to end, so they jump the gun and orchestrate the bumping into part of this new person knowing nothing might take off for a while.

For some people, connections take time before having full lift off where it's safe enough to bring them in and let it take its time evolving into more down the line. Meanwhile, the former love connection has fulfilled its contract agreement and begins to disband. It isn't long before the new love interest begins to have lift off.

This is one example of the many possible scenarios that can take place. There are times where no lift off happens due to free will choice. The connection will be pushed further and further out. Sometimes it never happens and one of the soul's passes on. Should the soul decide to have another Earthly life along with that soul mate at or around the same time, they will both be listed again on the new soul contract in hopes of recognizing one another. Therefore, some people might seem familiar to you, even though you just met them.

When two souls are ready and evolved enough, then the lifelong love partnership will happen when either least expects it. You will both be placed on the same path where it is orchestrated perfectly to the point, you're both standing face to face. There is no way either of you cannot see it.

The same is applied to work life and jobs. You could be stuck at what appears to be a dead-end job, but you have dreams of starting your own entrepreneurship, which is more popular today than ever in history. You may feel guided to leave your job, but you fear prevents you from making any changes. This can cause delays as well that may last for years. This isn't telling anyone to leave their job recklessly. It's something you must plan out methodically ensuring you are safe and secure enough to some degree.

If you have dreams of starting your own business, then take action steps today while at this job. You do this by devoting even just a half hour a day towards it when you're not at this day job. If you love this side business, then that passion and excitement will be the fuel for you to dive into on the side even when you're exhausted from your work at your regular job. You'd be surprised how devoting a tiny amount of time each day or week towards it starts to create some movement. When it's grown enough, then you'll know when it's safe to leave the day job. If not, then your Spirit team will yank you out of that job for this purpose. When you lose a job, you'll eventually see that it was for a reason. You are now free to work extra hard towards your life purpose work. This life purpose work and calling is one that is in your contract. The intense feeling you were receiving about leaving your job is your soul's awareness that this is something you are intended to do. You may not be aware of the origins of this feeling, but often it is something buried in your subconscious from soul memories of this contract.

All the experiences you have and will have in this life are part of your soul contract. They are all intended to contribute towards positively enhancing your soul and to bring you to the next step on your soul's evolving journey. Your Guide and Angel work with you in your life to ensure that you stay on the right path. Therefore, it's also important to be in tune and pay attention to your Guide and Angel. Staying on path is to help you fulfill the terms in your contract. When you're in tune and connected, it's not difficult to know what your purpose and terms are.

Sometimes you might be privy to what the terms are as circumstances happen for you. You might experience heartbreak in a love relationship and then say, "Now I know not to get involved with someone who is married and has no plans to leave their spouse."

You gained major soul and life enhancing skills in the process of the experience. It strengthened you to be on the lookout over who is a quality mate and who would not be good for you. These situations that happen can be in your soul contract. If it isn't, then it is the result of your free will choice, since no being in Heaven can intervene on your free will without your permission. Free will can cause an array of delays along your path, not to mention poor life choices. When you're not connected and in tune, but are guided by your ego and lower self, then you find that its one roadblock after another. You spend your entire life running around in circles chasing your tail doing what your ego wants. You may not come to the realization that this is what's happening until many years in. You discover, "Wow, what have I done the last five years?"

When your terms have been completed, you may exit this lifetime at that point, but not always. Sometimes one might fulfill their contract, but then will spend the remainder of their life working in a career that is their life purpose. They become of service to others or choose to spend their days enjoying their human retirement since they've fulfilled the terms in their contract. When you are in human retirement in later age you are still experiencing different kinds of purposes that could be connected to helping others in some way or gaining wisdom through study. The retired spent their life working hard on their life purpose and they deserve a break of luxury and relaxation too. Sometimes finally having that break is when they find their life purpose if it hadn't been discovered in the earlier years.

Luxury and relaxation are two qualities that Heaven wants to see all souls experience on a regular basis. They see relaxing and taking time outs as a necessity for your soul in order to recharge your soul's batteries. These acts are near non-existent today thanks to the break your back work all day everyday set up designed by the soulless. The soulful understand the benefits to working hard and smart, while also taking regular time outs. When you take regular time outs, breaks, days off, then you are more productive at work. You are stronger, healthier, and have a better attitude. This concept has yet to seep into the consciousness of many.

CHAPTER FIVE

Life Purposes

Every single soul on Earth has a list of life purposes in their soul contract. The purposes are all listed together in a pyramid like scheme. For example, one of my main life purposes is clear. It is my spiritual teaching work through the written word. Because this work was prominent in my life going back to childhood, it is listed at the top point of this pyramid. I had always subconsciously known this was what my Spirit team was leading me towards in a big way. As you sift downwards into the many layers of the pyramid there are an eclectic array of purposes within all of that, which are connected to the singular purpose. These might be things like working on being more fearless in certain areas of your life. I've had to personally work to master that over the course of my life considering that I'm a completely different person than I was when I was fifteen. I grew into my warrior like confidence as I entered my twenties.

One of your main life purposes is connected to what brings you and/or another person joy. It would also be what you would do for free if you had all the time and money in the world. Your life purpose is your passion that assists and benefits you as well as others. For instance, my writing work benefits a great deal of people as readers have reached out to me to share, but it also benefits me in that it's supremely therapeutic and helps me work out my own demons during the creative process.

If one's purpose is to live a life showering the world with love, then this is an objective that brings both you and another something positive. You could assign that example to an entertainer who enjoys being a musician and seeing people smile while they play on stage. In that instance they are showering the audience with love. You don't have to be a well-known entertainer that showers the world with love. You could be that neighbor who smiles and is warm and friendly with everybody on the block whenever you head outside. In that instance you are fulfilling one of your purposes of showering love on others.

God and your Spirit team know what your soul's life purposes are. They know what plans have been mapped out in your souls' contract for you. You also have this knowledge embedded deep in your subconscious too. It was something you agreed to before you chose to live an Earthly life. You can discover the answer to what that is when you tune in within. Your life purpose is not a question that can be answered by anyone, but yourself.

Not all life purposes are career related or a financial gaining one. Some life purposes are emotional traits learned, such as spending a lifetime learning how to easily forgive others over slights your ego feels they enacted on you. Forgiveness is one of the hardest action steps for a soul to reach, therefore this emotional trait exists in most every soul's contract on the planet. How do you forgive someone who took advantage of your good nature and seemingly destroyed an element of your life? It takes work and discipline to make your peace with someone that caused you turmoil. The sooner you do that, the quicker you evolve and move onto more important purposes. The angels and the egoless higher evolved spirits see the love in every soul, which is why they can exude the most magnificent forgiveness traits known to all creation.

Life purposes are easy to detect because it's one of the main goals that never seems to leave your mind throughout the years. For some, it is what gives you pleasure to dive into, but it can also be specific emotional traits that you struggle and wrestle with most of the days of your life, such as learning the act of giving, receiving, and to reducing anger and stressful dramatics to situations.

One life purpose example would be Albert Einstein and the work he contributed that assisted in prospering the planet. This doesn't mean all are called here to invent something. Many life purposes are geared towards acquiring soul enhancing traits such as gaining human life experience and the knowledge that it entails. This can be by learning responsibilities such as finding a job to pay your bills. There is more to Earthly life than finding a job and paying bills, but it's the learning responsibility act that is the knowledge gained that connects to your purpose. One should seek out a job that gives them pleasure and by default those around you. This isn't always an easy thing to do with the grave amount of competition fighting for the same role.

It's not uncommon to feel like you don't want to be here anymore or if you feel like your journey is complete. This is not always a fun world to live in. The misery created can be at the hands of those around you, but sometimes it can be you who is creating the misery without realizing it. If you're still here, then you are supposed to be, even if you have no clue as to why. It is your job and quest to discover why on your own. Ask yourself the important questions and examine your life to a hair-splitting degree to conclude as to why you are here. Everyone on the planet has a purpose.

In a journal or email to yourself, jot down the significant life events that transpired for you to date. What did you learn or gain from that? Allow your soul to involve itself in the Earthly life schoolwork so that you may graduate into other expanded spheres of soul consciousness. No one can do it for you. It's the same methodology as going to Earth's grade school. You had to show up to class, pay attention, study, and take tests in order to pass. Earthly life school for your soul is similar in that you must do the work, learn, grow, evolve, and graduate. You will be tested and asked to learn from mistakes you make or harm you've caused on other people, animals, and even the planet itself.

Earthly life is tough for millions of human souls that are working jobs that crush and kill their life force. Part of this is due to the current way that people have designed the modern-day work world. There is a greater distinction between working a job in a corporate environment you despise as opposed to finding a job that brings out your passions, creativity, and enjoyment. There are many souls that feel at home in a corporate structured environment, but it should be with the goal of making a positive impact for others. The problem is most that fall into that structure become equally rigid failing to invite in healthy balance. It's vital to your soul to balance your spiritual personal life and your practical work and career life.

As also discussed, not everyone's life purpose is ones chosen career. Many life purposes are not geared towards monetary success. Monetary success does not contribute to soul enhancing qualities, unless the millionaire is a humanitarian who uses their large income to assist those in need. This charity is an important character trait in enhancing one's soul.

A popular culture example could be someone like actress Angelina Jolie. She rose to movie stardom in the 1990's and into the 2000's and beyond. She was one of the final remaining true movie stars left before the rise of technology made everyone a star. She worked hard as an actress and her name became universally known, then she had that personal awakening moment while making the *Tomb Raider* films. The films were shot in beautiful countries that were also seeing hardship, refugees struggling, and poverty. This opened Jolie's eyes to the point that she once commented that it made her see life in Hollywood as trivial and superficial. Her new fight and larger purpose came to be her humanitarian work that never ceased and only continued to expand and grow over time. She became a United Nations Ambassador and Professor outside of her movie roles. The movie roles brought pleasure and entertainment to the masses, but one of the crucial elements it did per her divine soul contract was that it made her name popular and well-known. It was much easier for her to be taken seriously as a humanitarian and fight for those causes as a well-known name. Her big name would bring light to the tragedies happening in the world, because people will be more likely to see what Angelina Jolie is up to rather than a name they've never heard of.

I may not be of Angelina Jolie's universally known status, but my twenties were spent making a big name for myself behind the scenes in the film industry. Many in the entertainment business know who I am due to working with me over those many years, as well as the continued lifelong friendships I made with many in the business. I worked hard on film productions for the studios and talents in that industry, then like Jolie in a sense I also profoundly woke up towards the end of my twenties realizing that I was tired of the superficiality of the business. I remember working on a big film for Warner Bros. called *The Perfect Storm* at the young age of twenty-seven manning a crew of 800 people when I had another awakening moment. I was thinking, "I don't want to do this anymore. I love being here, but when am I going to start writing for a living?"

I had become in demand by the industry, but I wanted out. I wanted to follow my life purpose and become an author of work that helps the souls of humanity as per contracted. This feeling was something present in childhood and never left me, but towards the end of my twenties it was growing out of control that I couldn't shake it off. It propelled me to give up the high paying job offers to do what my soul was calling me to do knowing I'd be losing out financially. It wasn't about the money in the end. This is another clue as to what you're supposed to be doing. The feeling never leaves you throughout your life only growing bigger until you find a way to do it.

Not everyone fulfills elements in their soul contract. In fact, a great many number of souls do not fulfill it completely. This is one of the many long lists of reasons as to why some souls opt to come back for another Earthly life in order to fulfill the terms that were in the previous contract. Telling this to someone having an Earthly life now would prompt them to say, "Oh no, I'm not coming back here."

The ego part of us says that because the person's

current life experience or the state of the world today is not satisfying. It's filled with unhappy glum people that are also mean, heartless, and cruel. However, on the Other Side in Heaven, you have a much broader perspective. You're in a different space with far less ego. The soul wants to come back in order to fulfill its purpose or to assist the planet in a way that no other is doing. You realize back home that this is God's house and our job is to protect it.

Journalist, Oprah Winfrey, is a humanitarian that used her money to help others in a positive way. She opened the, "Oprah Winfrey Leadership Academy for Girls in South Africa". She's contributed millions of dollars over the years to help those suffering from poverty as well as towards others in making their dreams come true. She had an inner drive to do something positive with her life. She went after her dreams and achieved it. She then took the gift of monetary success and used it to help others in a positive way, which ultimately became her true soul's life purpose. This gave her and others joy.

This is one example of how to determine what someone's life purpose is. Your life purpose can be as big as being a friend to others the way Jesus was and is to the underdog. The irony being that many of his followers of today turn against or criticize the underdog, but so do people that have no belief system in place as well.

One's life purpose can be a side hobby that you enjoy doing. Brian, a twenty-six-year-old, set up a website to help people. This enabled others to email him for free advice. He has made himself an open door for others to discuss their problems with him. He doesn't charge anyone, but also doesn't care about that. He is fulfilled knowing he's been able to help at least one person. This is his life purpose. He discovered that it brings him, and others joy by being of service.

The world we live in requires that you must make money in order to survive. It's not like it was centuries ago when you could barter your services, which is giving someone something of value for something of value in return such as food and housing, etc. Over time human beings moved away from that and demanded that you use paper money for things. This gave money power over people. The ego in human souls will at times do whatever it can to obtain what they want. They will push others down to climb to the top of the ladder to stealing merchandise they want in a store to breaking into someone's car or property.

Greed has overpowered the human condition, which is also why bartering wouldn't survive today. You cannot trust humankind to be honest. There is nothing wrong with charging for your services as this is the way Earthly life is set up now. You cannot pay your rent with sticks and stones. You have to get a job to make money to pay for the necessities of life such as housing, transportation, clothes, and food.

In Brian's case, he has a day job, which is his primary source of income. If he deeply wanted to pursue his passion and life purpose full time, then he could begin requesting some measure of payment for his services, or like Churches add a donation button on his website. Never quit your day job to pursue your life purpose hobby unless it is safe enough to do so. This means your life purpose brings in enough income for you to survive so that you may safely leave your regular job. This is a dream that many would love to have. Not everyone wants to work in the rigid, cold, corporate environments. The way that Earthly life is set up now is that it's not as challenging to create your own business that is aligned with your purpose. Most everything is online now, and you can create businesses and services online without having to lease out a building to set up office. That's a major expense you're saving. There are some businesses that would require you to lease a space. An Esthetician wouldn't be able to work on someone's face unless the client is in the room with them. The Esthetician desires this kind of work. They are attracted to beauty and physical appearance upkeep. This is their life purpose because it brings joy to others through health, beauty, and self-care.

How can someone tell you what your purpose is? Only you know what brings you and others joy. This is for you to decide and not someone else. My life purpose is writing books and teaching through the written word. Not only does it bring me joy fulfillment, but I learned to understand that this has also been helping people around the world. To receive a note from someone in Turkey, Japan, or Australia who loved one of my books and had to tell me is cool. I'm happy to hear someone feels inspired in life after reading a piece of my work. This means the job that my Spirit team works to do is effective.

There is no need to worry that you've found a life purpose that isn't bringing in money. The key to knowing if it is your life purpose is if it brings you and/or someone else joy and assistance. You would do the work for free if you had all the time and money in the world. It's something you find yourself doing because you want to.

When you have free time from your day job, then you are excited to dive into your life purpose fun. Your life purpose doesn't feel like work to you. It's something you enjoy doing. Life purposes can also be helping the masses in some way such as working in a homeless shelter or traveling the world to assist those in need of basic lifesaving supplies. It can be painting on a canvas and showcasing your work in a gallery. Art brings others enjoyment; therefore, it is that artists life purpose. A concert performer enjoys putting on a show and the audience benefits by having a good time, which raises their soul's vibration. It takes them away from their mundane lives. This performing action is the band or singer's life purpose. Making movies that entertain and make people think a different way is a collaborative effort that is connected to all the filmmaker's life purpose. You will know it is your life purpose when you find that this is an activity you would participate in when you're not at your day job. It doesn't feel like work to you.

Everyone needs to be contributing something in

a positive way that is bringing love to another person. You were not born angry, bitter and depressed. Other human souls have inflicted that belief system on you. You absorbed it and reacted to it in ways where it might have permanently damaged you. It will be reversed and undone in this life or in the next when you pray and ask for heavenly assistance to lift those burdens off your soul. Invite in Heaven to permanently work with you on improving your life. They love you and want to help you reach a state of peace and contentment in your life.

One of your quests on learning to love is that you are tested repeatedly. This is done at the hands of those who may not be walking the talk, or who are not spiritual, but superficial. While you are working on your life purpose and contributing to humanity and your surroundings in a positive way, you may wonder what they are offering besides annoyance and grief. God, Heaven and the Angels see the love and your true self including the worst parts of your ego. Your criticisms and judgments are wasted words and energy.

Instead of reaching for that drink, I am more inclined to exercise. I'll jog up a mountain trail, or on the beach, or anywhere in nature. It is less stressful than jogging through the busy streets. I bike regularly along the beach coast as well. Exercise centers and elevates your spirit. You have more energy in the process while appearing and feeling better too! Others notice a brighter glow around you. Your entire aura and being attracts others to you. You have more time and energy during the day to accomplish important tasks. These tasks are geared towards your life purpose, spending quality time with loved ones, and more time for healthy rest. Relaxation is a luxury as well as a necessity. Get away for a couple of days and head to a place in nature, such as a park, the desert, the mountains or the beach where it is quiet and serene. I use those surroundings as an access to re-center myself if I am feeling out of sorts. If I'm at home and unable to get away for any reason I'll put on a melodic chill out or uplifting music album, then light some incense and candles. I will create a safe, calming sanctuary where I live.

Incidentally physical fitness trainers have a purpose that helps others get healthy and fit, while a massage therapist has the life purpose of contributing towards the health and well-being of their client through that act.

You are here to fulfill your life purpose, learn soul enhancing lessons, gain knowledge, and to enjoy this life and have some fun. This fun does not fall into the category of toxic. You are not asked to stop these poor ways of living for anyone's benefit, but your own. Heaven wants you to live at your fullest potential while experiencing euphoric feelings of joy. When you participate in healthy activities, exercise regularly, and have some measure of discipline about what you put into your body, then the fun and enjoyment you experience is beyond cosmic. If a stressful situation hits you, then as a high vibrational soul you can take on that stress in exhilarating stride. You are equipped to allowing the stress to roll off you without tampering with your energy field. The stressed situation evaporates rather quickly, than it would if you had not asked your Spirit team to intervene and work with you.

When you let go of all the burdens you carry on your soul by others, will you then see the truth of who you are. The obsession some have with homosexuality, race, politics and religion diverts the world from love, joy and their life purpose. You have a preoccupation over a breed of God's creation that you do not understand. Your ego and the infection of the Darkness allows this to happen preventing you from fulfilling terms in your contract. It is pushed to uproar out of fear and misguidedness. One of your life purposes is then to master that and learn how to come to terms with accepting others. If you are anti anything such as anti-gay, anti-race, anti-gender, but you want to evolve your soul, then it's time to begin the process of diving into what you despise so you can have a better understanding of it. More times than not, those that dive into understanding something they fear come out of it transformed and changed realizing they were previously misguided and wrong.

Whenever you do something good or bad this is filed away in your soul contract and records. Archangel Metatron who holds these records stands near the throne of God with the Archangel Jeremial during your life review. Your guide and angel are highly developed psychic entities that know your probable futures, your map, thoughts, feelings, and life purpose. They work to keep you heading in the right direction. You must tune in, pay attention, and communicate with them regularly, so that you stay on course and do not experience anger or sadness.

Don't shortchange yourself or be embarrassed as if you are not deserving of a great life. Heaven and your angels know you deserve it. They want you to be at peace, so that you can fulfill your life purpose. You do not have to be on this planet to suffer.

Your life purpose can also be whatever makes you angry or riles you up. For example, someone is always getting upset or angry when people throw trash in the ocean. This repeated anger for the same thing is a clue they were meant to come here to do something about it, such as joining in with an environmental organization, start a blog, or mobilize to clean up the oceans. This is their life purpose.

To turn your hobby into a career, take action steps towards it daily. You can do this in baby steps. Spend at least thirty minutes a day diving into whatever it is you want to accomplish. If you are working on a book, then spend at least thirty minutes each day writing a page. The universe will meet you tenfold in manifesting your dreams. When you are working on what you love, then it doesn't feel like a drag. You may be working at a job you're not happy with, but when you have something to look forward to at the end of the day, then it raises your vibration. This opens the door for the universe to step in and meet you halfway. You'll be that much closer to having your dream come true. It may feel like a struggle at first, but you will eventually notice the positive changes revealing itself to you in trickles over time. If you keep at it, then eventually that love will be your career! It will bring in enough financially that you're able to quit the job you're unhappy with. Ones hobby or love is often connected to their life purpose. However, a new human soul experiencing their first Earthly life may have a purpose that requires they learn patience or forgiveness. It might not be a specific "work" oriented goal, but it could be.

When you are not at your job, what do you enjoy doing on your off time? What is your hobby? Is it painting? Is it singing or playing the guitar? Your hobby is not surfing the internet, heading to the bar with friends every other night, or shopping for clothes. Those are called distractions, time wasters and addiction feeders at times. Your hobby is an activity that you enjoy doing on your own. It's one that gives you an added skill or knowledge around a certain area that gives you pleasure. Your hobby is what you want to turn into a career.

Let's look at a couple of well-known entertainers in music history. Bruce Springsteen has been playing his guitar since he was a teenager. When he was playing the guitar in those days it was his hobby and something he enjoyed doing. He was able to transition that hobby into a full-time career that lasted a lifetime. When entertainer Madonna was a teenager, she enjoyed dancing as a hobby. She took classes and looked for work that would enable her to incorporate her love for dancing. She was able to broaden that into an even bigger career that has also lasted a lifetime. Heaven applauds the music entertainers that bring joy to the world. Remove all the negative rants and criticisms that people whine about a musical artist they despise, then you will see a soul that enjoys being a musical artist and does it for the passion and love of it.

Many that work jobs that are not surrounding their hobby or passion are more likely to be unhappy than those who are. Those that are unhappy with their jobs tend to reach for addictions like alcohol, food or other toxic vices more than those who are happy with their work. Some of them reach for addictions to function. They will pop pills to tranquilize themselves to sleep at night and then ingest high doses of caffeine for an energy jolt to get them started every morning. You take something at night to calm down and sleep, and then you ingest something to infuse you with energy to get you going. The days where they are not at their job, like the weekend or a vacation day, they are less likely to reach for substances. This is a clue that you are unhappy at your job, but are convincing yourself that this is just the way it is.

If you keep making excuses that you're too tired or that you never have enough time, then you push your dream and purpose that much further away from you. The right time may never come unless you take control of your life by working this hobby into your schedule. I've had to work two full time jobs that included my regular job and my career. It can be done if everything in your entire being loves this hobby. You can turn this into a career if it is work that you are interested in doing as I did. Your finances are taken care of and you are completely settled and secure in every way. You are then able to spend time on this hobby because it gives you joy. The money that comes in from this work is just the icing on the cake. It is the benefits your purpose gives others which is its own reward.

CHAPTER SIX

Healing and Transformation

Every soul on Earth is evolving at varying paces and rates, including the ones that move at a slower rate. The ones moving through a slower rate of evolvement should be easily detectable since they're the ones that create the most havoc on the planet through the means of perpetual negativity and hatred. This can be visible in anyone from the violent to the lesser suspects, which are the ones that rant, complain, attack and rave on their social media accounts or to whoever will listen.

Hostility cannot be met with hostility. Hostility and aggression against someone whose values and thoughts don't agree with yours does not change minds or hearts. You cannot bully someone into submission no matter how much you despise their view or how much you feel their view is off. The bulldozing method to push them into submission is ineffective, meaning that it doesn't work. The human condition does not respond in kind to what it deems to be antagonism or a threat. The primal nature of human beings is similar to the animal kingdom where its first instinct is to react in defense of hostility. The soul consciousness is affected by all of this, but it is functioning on a higher playing field. It's a separate organism with a greater purpose than the physical primitive that weighs human life down.

The even lesser suspects are the seemingly nice people that have a strong attraction to gossip and superficiality. Those are the ones that base their existence on judging appearances. They are attracted to human labels that define and give the illusion of validity and popularity. They may do it innocently or superficially, but their soul's evolving process is at a similar motionless standstill as those below them such as the negative and violent attackers, whether through words or physical harm.

The souls that reside in the space of superficiality are higher up on that chain of evolving souls. They are closer to the precipice point of exceptionally evolving, but need that crucial awakening turning point that is more likely to come through over the lesser evolving souls. The lesser evolving souls are evolving, but it can take numerous lifetimes before it reaches the precipice of this transformational change of residing in love.

To break it down in simpler terms: 25% of the planet resides in the bracket of the slowest evolving souls. Those are considered the *baby souls*. They are the most dangerous due to the hatred they emanate off their auras. They are the ones completely taken over and held onto by the clutches of the Darkness. You know who those souls are since they are the ones that bully, harass, name call, attack, cause violence, and in other cases murder. It's all the same energy within that cluster of souls that will be transported into the same area upon death, which is through the back gate or left door of the darker part of the spirit worlds.

50% of the world is the dominant part of the planet filled with many souls that reside in the epicenter of superficiality. These are the *mid-level souls* what some might consider to be the average human being on Earth going through the motions, having an Earthly life, while repetitively obsessing and complaining over triviality. They would also be the ones that keep the gossip channels and social media business going through ranting and attacks. They may step into the role of perpetual complainer to whoever will listen whether in person or on social media. Social media dominates Earthly life today as the primary way of expressiveness and communication. One third of each of those two brackets of evolving souls will be or are on the precipice of evolving into the bracket above of them on the chain of soul evolvement.

The final 25% of the souls on Earth are the higher evolving souls filled with the most light. Those are the *evolved or evolving post graduate souls* that rapidly evolve into a higher consciousness during one lifetime. They are also easy to spot as those are the ones that are positively changing throughout the course of their life. They might be the ones that had that awakening moment while in the previous bracket of souls where they begin to question human life and the superficiality of it. They could've been that guy or girl that was obsessed with gossip and superficiality at one point, but suddenly begin to see things differently. They start to take a higher emotionally detached view of human life. They begin losing interest in the fads they were once interested in. They complain and rant less than they used to. Their emotional reactions to things grow calmer and more centered. They are the ones stepping into their higher purposes that have a positive global effect on humanity over time. Within those three core brackets you have the various levels of evolvement between each soul.

The higher evolving souls on Earth move through numerous healing and transformations in one lifetime, while a baby soul may only have one long lifetime of healing and transformation that becomes clear on their Earthly death bed. Going through a healing and transformation process can be tough as you shed the old former ways of your previous life, as well as any pain accumulated that has been lodged into your soul and aura. Healing and transforming is exceptionally beneficial because it contributes to your soul's growth. You go through some rough stuff in your life, and as a result you come out of it smarter and stronger.

This doesn't mean it's necessarily fun going through all of that, but it is obligatory. If you don't experience challenges, then you don't grow. If everything is handed to you, then you risk becoming spoiled and entitled.

Healing and transforming doesn't have a timeline attached to it. It's an individual experience that can take months to years as the soul is evolving away from a certain experience. Take your time working through any healing and the emotions associated without rushing it. Avoid falling into any paths of toxic addictions to numb the pain. All that does is put a temporary Band-Aid on it before you're eventually thrown back to the beginning where you recall the healing you were originally going through. You still must allow that healing to take place, which will then propel you into the transformation stage.

During those stages you might across feelings of loneliness and isolation. When that happens reach out to others that understand what you're going through. Connect with open-minded friends that can empathize and be sympathetic. There are also support groups you can join where there are likeminded individuals going through the same thing. It doesn't feel so lonely and is more familial and full of community. When going through a personal transformation you may find that you cannot relate to anybody, which is perfectly standard and normal as your soul is awakening and your consciousness is being raised in the process.

This nineteen-year-old reader once mentioned that the images I've sometimes used for a social media posting tend to have only one person in them and that it seemed to symbolize loneliness. Although an interesting observation, the reasoning is because one's spiritual quest is a solo experience. When your soul is wounded, the first place it shows up is in relationship connections. One of the goals of the soul mates around you is to awaken something in you that needs to be addressed or caressed to life. The positive side to the more super intimate relationships you have is to help you see what needs to be dealt with within you or positively opened up. It's still an individual soul experience that is being enhanced by those around you regardless if the soul mate is a friend, acquaintance, colleague, or love relationship.

You may have been attracting in the same types of people into your world or you have had the same types of friendships for years, then one day you go through a major transformation and suddenly you are no longer attracted to the kinds of people you normally were. When this happens, then your energy vibration has lifted causing a change on the path you've been on where it's raised and then shifted upwards. You'll know which direction it went in by the kinds of energy that new circumstances end up being based in. When you grow, evolve, change your perception, and work to raise your consciousness, then you can be assured that many of your surrounding connections will change.

I've sifted through so many different levels of energy vibrations over the years that those I hung around with also changed. There are the loyal friendships in my circle that have been around me for decades, because they also personally shifted while being open to the changes I was going through as I with them. Others moved into the acquaintance box where we would remain in touch, but we were not as tight the way we once were on a regular basis. They are good people, which is why we still connect on occasion, but our views and personalities went in different directions.

Life continues through these interpersonal shifts that move like the tides in the ocean. The soul consciousness is a fascinating energy as it fluctuates, grows and evolves over the course of a lifetime. Then you have other soul consciousness beings on the planet that never grow. They remain exactly at the same intelligence level they were at when born. Those consciousness beings continuously die only to be re-born again in another Earthly life in hopes of getting that soul consciousness to expand and evolve out of the clutches of the Darkness.

Your current existence might throw you some wild curve balls where you were heading down one path, but then something offsets it and you're suddenly going down another road. This doesn't mean the road is necessarily worse than the one you were already on. Neither were bad roads, but something poignant takes place that upsets the balance and you're re-directed down another path that in hindsight is potentially better than what you previously had in mind.

Born into Abuse, Bullying, and Trauma

Rough life circumstances you endure will improve over time since nothing stays the same forever. It's tough at first, but as trite as it sounds, time does heal the painful wounds and struggles you go through during the soul's crushing phase. This is the case even if you recall certain incidents that surround what caused the pain to begin with. It's not met with the same severity it had when the healing process began. You become stronger and a force to be reckoned with because of it.

Many born into abuse, bullying, or any kind of trauma tend to be stronger than others because of those experiences they were forced to endure. The dangers for some are if the damage is so great that the soul has a hard time being lifted to do the work of going through the healing and transformation process. As a result, they could end up caught in a permanent victim position where their life seems to be stuck on pause. You want to do the work to understand why horrible traumatic circumstances took place by moving away from blaming anyone. You may have been in a prolonged child abusive situation, but this is what is also giving your soul the accelerated growth and evolving God had in mind for you for a greater reason.

Work hard to move forward fearlessly down that opened road in front of you. In the beginning, it is human nature to place blame and fault on someone else that hurt you or slighted your ego. You want to reach that place where you forgive them, so that you can let go of what happened and move forward to the next plateau. Forgiving them doesn't mean you're making excuses for their actions. Their actions will feel unforgiveable because it was so detestable and caused pain to you or others. The abuser will meet their karma later and have to answer to that and pay it back in this lifetime, the Other Side, or the next. That will not be your problem or your issue to concern yourself with. You will forgive them for you, so that you don't have to carry around that toxicity, weight, and burden that someone else created.

You endure the varying levels of emotions one must go through when healing and transforming. This includes understanding what brought the circumstances on to begin with. This is whether it was personal choices or a free will choice that led to the event happening.

Other considerations are if you were powerless to have been in an upsetting situation. This can be where you were a child born into a home of abuse and under the power of someone else as I was. It wasn't a personal choice you made to be there, but you were born into it. There are several reasons this could have happened. One is that the soul chose to be born in a turbulent environment for a specific gain or advantage that is understood to be at a later date. This might be hard to be believed at the time. The flip side is the parent or parents operated on free will choice and from the Darkness that got a hold of them to control their ego. You didn't ask for it, because no one asks for horrific abuse.

I grew up in a violently abusive household where I endured abnormally cruel psychological, emotional, and physical abuse by a parent. All my earlier relationship love partnerships ended due to the person either being uncommitted or they strayed to the point where I ended up trusting no one. I'm on guard with anyone new I come across as I automatically expect poor behavior to be displayed since nine times out of ten that winds up happening. People have an ulterior motive to attempt to control or oppress. This isn't the case with the enlightened higher evolving ones. This is the cliff note version of what took place to illustrate that I understand how challenging it would or could be to reach that place where you can forgive. You forgive your abusers for your soul's benefit, because you don't want to carry that trauma and anger around for the rest of your life. You have other work to do and you wish them well on their path.

What all those people did at the time was not okay, but like me you will spend years letting it go and releasing it. While there is no feeling of animosity, there are remains that I'm stuck with such as the occasional PTSD reactions that pop up out of nowhere or the permanent social anxiety. You learn to orchestrate your life that is conducive to your well-being temperament.

As you let go of past trauma and work through it, then you grow stronger and wiser. Your vibration rises, your soul consciousness expands, you get healthy, and you start to pay more attention to your Spirit team. You allow yourself to feel them, exercise more, hydrate, watch what you consume since that can affect one's feelings. High amounts of caffeine can heighten anxiety, while drugs or alcohol can give rise to depression feelings. Work on seeing things with a positive outlook. Circumstances happen for a reason and although that reason is not seen immediately, over time it is revealed as to why one endured a situation that called for healing and transformation.

Sometimes helping others or being of service to those in need is a positive way to get through healing. It moves your focus away from what's going on inside you and towards the donating of one's time in assisting others. It's therapeutic for one's self as well, because sometimes you're guided to help those who are in similar situations. Many great healers fall into that role because they might have had to endure past trauma or abuse. They know how to successfully navigate past that in order to help others. They have more sympathy and compassion for their patients or clients because they too had to endure that. This doesn't mean there are no healers who did not endure that either. They might be an Earth Angel with empathic psychic gifts of walking in someone else's shoes to get to the root of an issue.

Lead by Example

Transforming your soul includes evolving in order to see the broader picture. This helps in stripping away the ego, which causes most of the sabotage. When you view most things from the perception of an egoless being, then you receive that clarity. There are numerous soul lights threaded around the world doing what they can to offer reminders of the soul's path and to help other souls evolve. This may come in the form of correcting disrespectful behavior, teaching compassionate common-sense etiquette, helping someone through suffering, teaching positive spiritual concepts, helping others have a more peaceful and content life, giving and displaying love, shining at your brightest, and allowing those in the vicinity to soak that up. None of that is without its challenges. You're dealing with those who have an exceptionally stubborn, rigid, limited consciousness and can only see what they've been taught to date. It is rare for a human soul to branch away from how it was raised and follow their own path, since most follow what they've been taught or directed to do. There is only so much you can do to help. The best way to assist is to lead by example since you cannot force someone to bow to your whim. Not only is that against the *Universal Free Will Law*, but some souls will remain at the consciousness level they are currently at through one Earthly lifetime.

Earthly life is a school freely open for any soul looking to evolve and grow. The mediocre minds on Earth have made fun of others who seem to be buried in a book. We've seen this in Hollywood films about teenagers where there is always that one teenager making fun of the friend with books in her or his hand.

"Why are you bringing your books?"

The one carrying those books will be going far in life we can assure you. Immersing yourself into study and research to raise and awaken your consciousness in order to transform has a greater long-term investment on your soul than staying where you are.

Transform and Evolve

The Archangel Nathaniel tends to show up in someone's life when that person is going through a major transformation. He assists in removing anything outdated one after the other. This can include work, love, friendships, etc. It's a huge elimination, purging, and cleaning process that's taking place. This is in order to begin moving you into a new and better chapter with no additional baggage. This new chapter is more like a new book because the soul's perception of circumstances also shifts and expands as well.

Archangel Nathaniel's energy is perfect with mine as he's quite aggressive, heated and passionate in a way. He can intimidate those that might be too sensitive to that kind of energy, but I've always felt at home working with him.

Evolving souls have been choosing to incarnate since Earth's conception. At the turn of the 20th Century and beyond, the numbers of incarnations have increased astronomically to match the demand for human life choosing to procreate at an astronomical rate into the billions. This is due to poor sexual indiscretion, ignorance, peers push them to, ego rule, or because they believe God tells them it's what they're supposed to do. All are equated with the lack of soul knowledge because God doesn't instruct anyone to overrun the planet to the eight billion and growing mark. The more human souls multiply, then the more Earthly realm souls choose to incarnate.

You may be stuck in the in-between stage of being a non-evolved soul to an evolved one, which is what the Mid-Level Souls are enduring. They are at the precipice of knowing there is much more than the mundane Earthly life than finding a job, getting married, buying a house, and having kids. An understanding is rising that there is something deeper going on with the Universe beyond what human civilization set up for physical survival.

You could be experiencing confusing and conflicting emotions about the world and wondering why you are here. You have your own personal identity that is in a tug of war with the ego part of you that wants to feel important. You will do whatever it takes to obtain this. This doesn't change as you continue to transform, unless some measure of self-awareness has seeped into your consciousness. In God's eyes you're already important without the desire for domination.

Throughout Earth's history, humanity has continuously seen one challenging year after another unable to break free from that cycle. This is on a global level, while the individual part of you is attempting to figure out who you are and what your purpose and place is currently. You may be searching for your own identity and wrestling with the meaning of life. Some will follow what their caregivers have instilled in them, while others will break away from that and assert their individuality to become an independent thinking human being. No matter how much you attempt to break away from what your caregivers have instilled in you, there will be traces of what your caregivers have placed upon you. It can take a lifetime to diminish the learned traits you're not proud of. You are evolving in that process. The loudest unheard voices come from the evolved. Be your own champion and walk with the Light.

A familiar theme among those touched by the Light is they are initially on the wrong side of humanity. They are visited by a spirit, which results in a life changing transformation from within. In one chapter of the infamous book *The Christmas Carol*, the greedy Scrooge miser directs his anger at the Spirit of the Present. Scrooge condemns God and all that work in his name for humankind's bad behavior. He cowers when the Spirit rises over him and lashes out with the truth straight up and as bold as the Mighty.

"There are some upon this earth of yours who lay claim to know us, and who do their deeds of passion, pride, ill-will, hatred, envy, bigotry, and selfishness in our name, who are as strange to us and all our kith and kin, as if they had never lived. Remember that, and charge their doings on themselves, not us!"

Author Charles Dickens would forever be praised for Divinely channeling what would become a profoundly philosophical message disguised in the tightly organized Christmas Carol. Academics would spend their life debating whether the piece was a non-religious story or a Christian metaphor. Considering that it's historically attracted people on both sides and everyone in between since it came out all those centuries ago indicates it's spiritually Universal.

Scrooge is a narcissistic cold hearted mean selfish man who is given a forced life review in the middle of the night. I call it *Spirit Hours* because you're not distracted and instead are receptive to receive. Scrooge is first visited by his deceased business partner Jacob Marley. Marley is stuck roaming the Earth with heavy chains and money chests weighing his soul down in the Darkness. He warns his old friend of the same fate and much worse if he doesn't repent and change his ways. This is followed by Scrooge being visited by three spirits, which would've been an order of angels and High Spirits, with the goal of freeing him from bondage of the ego's self while simultaneously transforming him into joyful deliverance.

This metaphor of the Christmas Carol would be a sign that you're transforming and evolving as Scrooge did. You're moving away from the familiar old and into the confident brightness of the new.

Transcending Utopia

Transcending utopia means to go beyond your limits and travel outside of the generic mundane materialistic achievement that human beings taught one another to thrive for. A utopian society is what every soul secretly longs for deep down. It is where everything is perfectly blissful on all levels according to the core soul values you were born with. It isn't just outwardly perfect, but the sensations connected to how flawless everything feels reveals the authentic perfection that you were made from. Utopia is the ideal paradise as imagined in one's dreams that is also unachievable by human standards. Heaven and all the spirit realm worlds on the Other Side contain the highest forms of Shangri-La, but to get close to that experience while on Earth requires a soul adjustment.

Transcending utopia is a state of mind that all spirit beings long for you to have. For some it is easy to achieve if your natural disposition state is pleasant and enjoyable, even during stressful times. It is having everything you ever dreamed of to the degree of being completely content in all ways and on all possible levels that your being has the potential for. Transcending utopia is going beyond that and even further into the distant reaches of the Universe that are impossible for the lower mind to achieve. Never give up, never lose faith, and keep forging on fearlessly towards that goal of continuous soul consciousness transformation.

CHAPTER SEVEN

Soul Groups and Earth Angels

There are three core human soul groups as mentioned in the previous chapter:

• Baby Souls. Those are the souls causing the greatest harm on Earth. They use the maximum amount of darkness of ego. They're the ones that harm, hurt, or hate. They start wars, incite violence, and destruction on the planet or on other beings. Many are the criminals on Earth, but there are also souls who are not criminals, yet cause quite a bit of heartache or disaster on others through words towards others as well too.

• Mid-Level Souls. Those are the ones just trying to get by and survive. They are trying to make it through an Earthly life. Their purposes are geared towards working hard on one or many aspects of themselves. They may be on the planet to live an Earthly life and follow the human customs of that time such as getting a job, getting married, buying a house, having kids, etc. Some of them may reside in the epicenter of superficiality and gossip or attention seeking. At some point one of these souls may start to question life in general and possibly receive an awakening that thrusts them to graduate and begin moving to a higher soul level.

• Evolved/Evolving Post Graduate Souls. These are the teachers or the ones bringing light and wisdom to others on some level. They enact positive change and tend to steer clear of the human ego trappings as much as possible. Some of them may be greatly evolved and here to live an Earthly life while bringing something positive to the planet. There will be other souls who are evolving out of the Mid-Level Soul branch and into this branch during their lifetime. Those are the ones also living several lifetimes in one. Many souls from the various realms that exist on the Other Side incarnate as an evolved or evolving soul to offer their services to the betterment of humanity, but may start out in the Mid-Level soul branch, even though deep down there is a deepness old soul like quality about them from as far back as childhood.

Human Souls Operate on Different Levels

On Earth, there are hierarchy positions within some companies running from the CEO down to the executives, to the assistants, receptionists, and so on. What is interesting is that even though a CEO on Earth may be financially successful, they could be spiritually bankrupt. Their Earthly drive is for monetary success and nothing else. They could be considered a baby soul in the spiritual world, while their assistant may be a realm soul that Heaven knows to be an evolved/evolving, advanced, post-graduate soul, which in the end is what lasts beyond your time on Earth. Only on Earth is the distribution of power imbalanced or what human souls consider to being of power, since real power is spiritual soul competence.

A parent might be a baby soul ruling from the darkness of ego, while their child could be an evolving post-graduate soul that is much older in soul years than their own parent. This would be obvious where the parent seems to be more childlike with its abusive nature and/or tantrums, and the child comes off more wise, centered, or compassionate than its parent.

All human souls will die and when that happens, they will be buried just like every other human being that passes on. They will be buried without anything, but what they're dressed in. Even that will tarnish and grow old over time covering a physical body that disintegrates into the Earth's ground before becoming a set of bones. The soul that continues to live on will exit that body and immediately move towards the part of their soul's home with other souls that are of a similar equitable nature. There is no such thing as power to get ahead in Heaven, because all souls live in peace and harmony. They're not fighting or killing one another off to get ahead.

Upon human death, the assistant that worked on Earth moves to a higher space of consciousness than the CEO on Earth did due to him not growing his soul consciousness while here. This is because in the spirit realms you move to areas where your soul group is. The soul group consists of your soul siblings that have similar gifts as you do and who are on the same soul growth level. You head back home to Heaven upon your Earthly death with newfound insight you gained while on Earth.

Living an Earthly life you are forced to engage with souls that are on various levels of soul growth that may be similar or dissimilar to you. What is immediately understood for you is the chaos that ensues on the physical world. Many souls on Earth struggle to get ahead and one up each other to prove they have the answers when in reality few have only slices of truth.

Human beings ruling their life from the darkness of ego cause most of the misery experienced. If every single soul on the planet were in tune and connected with the Divine full time while using their God given born traits of love, then Earth would be as blissful as Heaven. This will unlikely happen since Earth is filled with Baby Souls. Those newborn souls that sparked out of God were quickly born into a human body for the sake of learning and growth on Earth.

Children throw tantrums when they don't get what they want, and baby souls are no different. A baby soul can be in the body of a 70-year-old human being. Just because the human being is appearing of older age it does not mean they're wise. It is still a baby soul who has experienced one lifetime at this Earth school. Depending how rapidly they evolved will determine where they will go upon their exit of the human vessel.

Some Earthly souls will display a higher range of their gifts than other souls, but it doesn't mean that other souls are incapable of that. All souls are the same inside as they came from the same Light. If they display less of the gift than another, then this is connected to having a block in the physical world, or it is compensated through having an ability displayed through another gift that someone else might have less of. All are born into an Earthly life with specific psychic gifts that are extra enhanced than another for them to use that for the purpose of the higher good. This benefit is also for them to pay attention to so that they can be guided along their Earthly path with minimal challenges as possible.

All souls will endure challenges as that is the nature of the beast that is the Earthly life. Those more in tune to the planes beyond will work harder to access their deep gifts in order to be able to move about through any Earthly challenges swifter than someone else who ignores those gifts.

Earth Angels

Lucifer was a fallen angel that once resided in Heaven. He was magnificently beautiful looking and made this incredible music sound wherever he moved. One day he decided to defy the Light in a big way and was cast out of Heaven due to the corruption he was attempting to create. It's important to note that he chose to be cast out. He had that choice because God doesn't keep any prisoners or anyone that doesn't want to be there, regardless if it's an angel or human being. We're not puppets on strings that God is playing and controlling. All souls have free will choice to do something good or choose to do something bad. Lucifer made the latter choice time and again that his soul was drawn out of Heaven since the Light spits that stuff out if it's contaminated. He fell like a lightning bolt and now resides in what some refer to as a fiery pit of Hell. Some belief systems believe there is this fiery pit with Lucifer looking like a red ogre with a tail and pitchfork that has become a popular culture image, especially during Halloween time and in scary films. This is not what he looks like as he's quite exceptionally beautiful looking, but his soul is hideously dangerous. This is how he can cause such deception to the ego mind, because the ego is pulled in by someone's attractive exterior instead of what's in the soul's heart.

Earth is one of the dimensions of Hell. This means that Lucifer is not actually below the Earth, but here on Earth. He is technically located in one of the layers of Hell located between Earth and

Heaven. This is one of the additional explanations of why I have Clairvoyantly seen these creepy crawlies and other darker entities spilling into the Earth plane since childhood. I could never understand that throughout my adolescence until the missing pieces to the puzzle were being shown to me by my Spirit team over the course of time. Then I was mesmerized as if I had discovered gold, "Ohhhhhh. Wow. That's interesting."

Lucifer is close enough to create destruction in the lives of human beings. He does this because he can. He wants power the way some human beings desire greed and power. It isn't for the purpose of good, but the purpose of annihilation and ruin. He works through them to push them to accomplish this through simple manipulation and influence. It's like taking candy from a baby it's so easy.

Earth is owned by God, but the Devil is temporarily running it by infecting anyone he can. It's not just through vitriolic hatred and violence, but he can do this through selfishness, greed, and self-centeredness. He invades people's minds by poisoning it. He can do little deceptive things such as whispering into your consciousness that you're no good at anything. He'll crush your self-esteem, because he enjoys belittling and bullying others. He'll also do that through other people by contaminating and influencing them to behave badly with others. These are the ones that are predominately bad, rather than the rare moment a genuinely good person is stressed out about something.

Examine how many people believe the negative thoughts about themselves. No Light being will ever talk to you the way the Darkness does. The Devil will steal souls to create a growing army of Darkness in the Hell regions, including on Earth which is evident. Your soul can choose to live in the Light which will take that power away from the Darkness. The most difficult ones he can't get into easily are those of the Light on Earth.

Earth is one of Lucifer's dominions where he has some of the most success at rallying, enslaving, and masterfully manipulating millions of souls every second all at once. He plagues the planet by working through them. They form into Locusts that spread and urinate lower energy wherever possible. To counter that God sends His trusty light warriors to contribute their parts at tempering and stomping that darkness out as much as possible. We sometimes call these lights Earth Angels that incarnate from another land beyond the veil, but even they can be susceptible to the lower energy if they're not careful. They are gifted and capable of wiping it away as quickly as possible and getting right back to work with their exceptionally keen focus, drive, and purpose. God only sends His best, which only angers the Darkness like you would never believe. God's best are a thorn in the side of the Darkness.

The Light warriors tend to be highly sensitive in some way, as well as profoundly psychic more than those that are unaware of their psychic abilities. They are more in-tune to the vibrations beyond the physical plane due to the many previous life lessons they've gained. The harder the life lesson the stronger your evolving process is. The more you evolve the clearer your consciousness. The clearer your consciousness the keener your psychic channels are.

The Light souls on Earth do their best to stay away from anyone that resides in a lower energy space. They can detect when to steer clear due to having a vastly tuned-in calibrated psychic antennae. They move towards those that reside in a higher vibrational Light state, while the darker human soul attracts in others that reside in a negative space. Their negative energy grows more repressed as the Dark energies take over, while the stronger sensitive soul rises like helium above the Darkness and into the vortex of the Light where love resides.

One of the few traits that all Earth Angels have in common is that they're keenly aware they are here to do His will. This is the common link that brings them all together in a communal circle like the Avengers fighting crime. Each brings their distinctive personalities and talents to their holy rampage with the goal of protecting and progressing humanity and the planet.

Some higher evolved souls will continue to incarnate into an Earthly life beyond their final incarnation. They are not doing that for the purpose of balancing out any Karmic debt or for soul growth purposes, even though the positive side effect is additional soul growth. This is never shunned by an intelligent consciousness. They desire to contribute something positive towards humanity that can benefit the planet.

Many of the higher evolved souls are the warriors of lights, light workers, and earth angels that all view the planet as God's home and creation that needs protection. It's like when someone housesits for a best friend. They treat the home as if it is their own. Because they are protectors of His work, they have a deep desire to keep the planet healthy on His behalf. Relying on newborn souls to keep it in great shape is not an option, because when you put a tantrum havoc-wreaking child in a room, then you cannot expect it to clean that room up. You might walk into that room to find it is in complete disarray with crayon writing on the wall.

The child needs to be trained and taught that destroying a room is not appropriate behavior. The child that resists knowledge ends up having a harder life. Every soul on the planet has the soul capacity for great knowledge gained including the tantrum child. They need higher evolved souls or evolving souls to guide and teach them. We see these higher evolved souls in the people around the world that are making positive differences in the lives of human beings. Some of these highly evolved souls may not even be cognizant of their role. They enjoy what they do so much that the deeper meaning and quest behind what they're doing isn't on their radar.

It is easier for a higher evolved soul to accomplish those tasks while in a human body, rather than attempting to do it in a spirit body that many don't pay attention to. Most people either have trouble accessing God, Spirit, the Angels, Higher Spirit Beings, or they don't believe in it. Irrespective of anyone's personal human belief system this lifetime, every soul has the gifts of Divine communication.

Higher evolved souls view the constant chaos on Earth from Heaven as all souls do through the veil. Gradually some of them conclude that they must incarnate into a human body for a specific cause that can help progress Earthly life positively in some way. If the higher evolved souls never choose to come to Earth, then Earth will eventually be destroyed. It's like the abandoned home that is soon ruined and destroyed by trespassers that have no consciousness. If you think Earth is in a poor state now, then imagine if the souls of the Light that are here now trying to temper that decided not to come here. Earthly life would end up in ruins and destroyed. Things like there would be no human laws enacted to capture criminals and keep them locked up to prevent further destruction. Even though it is true some of the laws are warped and criminalize people that are not truly criminals. They might have committed a crime that would be considered minor in Heaven's eyes, as opposed to a larger true crime such as grand theft, murder, assault, or physical harm and violence to another person or property.

The danger for the higher evolved soul that incarnates into a human life is they are as susceptible to the negative energies as anyone else. They can succumb too deeply to Earthly pleasures that could prevent them from getting to work. I know this well since my spirit has experienced everything under the sun, around the block, and back again. Keeping it balanced is significant to guarantee you don't get lost in it to the point that months have passed by and you realize, "Wait a minute I haven't accomplished anything good."

That was a statement I had made during my adolescent stage more than once. This doesn't mean I was never exempt from behaving what some might consider badly. I grew up this lifetime as a rebellious reckless aggressive warrior soul. Wanting to get my hands onto anything that was toxic. Temptations have never been beneath me in the past. If I had never tried it before, then I wanted to. Some of it was for me to escape the pain I was experiencing in this life due to the repetitive childhood trauma, but some of it was also to experience so that I could have a better understanding of it and report back. All the colors on my soul's palette were bright and receptive to it all. At the same time, I was fearless despite all the warnings of those around me that I shouldn't do certain things. If I shouldn't do it, then I would.

I may be highly in tune psychically, but I'm also a former addict to anything and everything I could get my hands onto. Our human lives are always met with some measure of turmoil. Even the ones you think who have everything down or who have it together are not exempt from this. They also have lessons they're wrestling with since no one gets a free pass.

The higher evolved soul may choose to incarnate for a specific purpose that contributes something awesome to human life. If they're going to take the time to incarnate and live a human life to be able to accomplish this, they will add other elements in their soul contract to achieve while at it. They might choose to live a harder life for a brief period that will help their soul adapt to the harsher aspects of Earthly life. This way they can gain important disciplined traits they need to help them accomplish their purpose or purposes. The soul is aware before incarnating that the risk of their Earthly mission is that their soul's memories of Heaven and their psychic channels will be suppressed and potentially diminished once in a human body. This is why many human beings tend to have amnesia about where their soul came from or what it's like back home in Heaven.

Over time there will be souls on Earth that begin to remember or discover ways that can help re-open their psychic channels they're born with. I've talked about many of those methods throughout my work. Much of what my Spirit team has filtered through me to discuss isn't to ruin someone's Earthly pleasurable fun or to condemn troublesome behavior that can backfire on you. It's to offer what helps in awakening those psychic clair senses that is more connected to God than anything else. Having a strong faith-based system makes life a bit easier than not having that faith. God is your long-term family unit and you want Him on your side. Everything my Spirit team teaches is also for me too. I'm certainly not exempt from this. During my adolescent immature phase, I disregarded what they'd teach the way any teenager scoffs and disregards what their own parents are attempting to instill in them. As I was growing older, I was still aware of what my Spirit team had been teaching me and was beginning to adopt much of what they had been teaching. I realized what they were helping me with was on the mark, so I began to share that with others that were interested too.

CHAPTER EIGHT

The Earthly Birth

Heaven, the Spirit World, and the Other Side are all the same place depending on whom you talk to and how that soul prefers to label it. You are a soul in a human body living an Earthly life for a numerous chain of purposes. Some souls have many intentions, while others have one big objective above those intentions. There are also universal goals, which include learning to love or bringing others together in a positive way. If you were born to love and that comes innately, then you are a teacher of love. You lead by example in expressing that love full time naturally. This is because your gifts are stronger in the areas of your purpose. It doesn't take much work to use them, but it does take work to put them to action.

Into the lighter doorways of the spirit worlds, there is no darkness or pain, no judgment or criticisms, no hatred or violence. There is no ego therefore no greed or resistance, any power or repressed oppression. It is a utopian wonderland filled with enormous beaming light and flickers of vibrant sparkles of color that moves in the direction you will it to be. This Light reaches anything that can be filled from every soul, cell, plant, desert, mountain, ocean, or animal on all planes and dimensions that exist throughout time and space. You may call this light God, a Higher Power, the Source, Spirit, the Light, or any other name comfortable to the current reality your consciousness has chosen today. Unlike human life it has no desire for labels because in Heaven this Light just IS. Names and labels are what human beings use in order to differentiate, describe, or single out something that desires no separation back home. When I use a label, it is so that one can have a quick understanding of what we are talking about, but otherwise they're not part of Spirit's vocabulary.

The Light affects all that it touches with the same positive results. It brings on a sensation of overflowing love, peace, and joy. It consumes you in a magnificent way bringing with it an out of this world uplifting sensation that can make one feel as if it's going to fall over or burst apart while in it. It's an exhilarating high that cannot be obtained by any human made drug, food, or drink on Earth. If you've ever been in love with someone that loves you back, then you understand the rush of excitement and joy that is experienced when you both physically touch one another to sitting alone in one another's presence. This is because love in any form releases your soul from the confinement it suffers through while having an Earthly life. This same rush of excitement that comes from a lover's touch is magnified one hundred times on the Other Side just by being in Heaven's atmosphere. It feels like you're soaring even when you're standing still.

When your soul steps into this Light, then any negative feeling you're experiencing is blasted away immediately. When a soul crosses over to the next plane passing the dark exits and through the right doorway and front gate, it then enters this Light where all emotional, physical, or mental deterioration that soul was battling with on Earth diminishes. If you had what you consider to be a handicap or any kind of physical or mental disorder or disability, then this is removed and exists no longer as your soul travels through the rays punching through the doorway of Light. Any kind of human handicap or disorders are an Earthly physical condition connected to the physical body vessel you're temporarily renting before you vacate your premises, but it is not the true state of your soul. Therefore, you want to avoid singling yourself out with labels such as having a disease or handicap that you identify with unless it's relevant to a cause you're fighting for.

"Hi, I'm Mary and bound to a wheelchair because...."

Or, "Hi, I'm Bob and I'm HIV Positive."

It may be a physical human disease or handicap that has attacked your physical body this lifetime, but it is separate from the core part of your soul that ends up erased from your consciousness when your spirit travels back home. Who you currently are would be Mary or Bob, a loving and compassionate soul who gives to others generously through your empathetic activism.

If you own a car, you do not say, "Hi I'm so and so, I drive a BMW and I work for a law firm."

You are not the car you drive or the job you work at, regardless that these are the physical, material, external things that people focus on. When one meets someone new, they immediately go down the generic list of human taught questions such as, "What do you do for a living? Where do you live? Where are you from?"

Those are temporary identities you've assigned to your physical being, but have no validity once you vacate your vessel. It's just something you are choosing to affiliate with today at this point in your life, but your roles on Earth do not define you. Who your soul is back home is what defines you beyond any temporary physical attributions and statuses.

Your soul sometimes chooses a handicap in order to develop a different perspective or for a specific purpose or goal that the soul must discover on its own. The challenges of this handicap contribute to soul enhancing and growth properties that the soul might otherwise not gain if they were not having that experience.

To my ego mind, I could express doubt, but to

my higher self's space and what my team relays, I receive it with an open mind and disburse the information publicly by allowing others to decide for themselves what they're comfortable accepting to be of truth. Doubting partially comes from the ego part of a soul not wanting to believe something is possible or for real. Doubts are concerns and worries where you require additional concrete visible answers that will bring your ego to a higher level of comfort and peace. It adds security to ease the skeptical questioning part of you, but your higher self has no doubts. Doubts can also signify a warning nudge from your Spirit team preventing you from heading into danger. When you cross over back home your soul and physical self is restored to top form appearing around in the ranges of a human being aged twenty-five to thirty-five, but in a more profoundly radiant way than visibly imaginable. Some souls may temporarily appear to be the age they passed away at to a clairvoyant medium in order to be recognizable to you.

On Earth, someone might have a cup of coffee to wake up in the morning, or they might have a glass of wine or a beer to wind down after a long day at work. Sometimes they do this to let loose and have some fun since the life they currently live feels joyless, stressful, and restricting. There is little to no love experienced in one's life. When you're high in love, you rarely yearn for a drink or drug. This Light in Heaven is your cup of coffee or bottle of beer. You do not crave a vice back home in Heaven. The state you attempt to achieve while living an Earthly life through vices is reached naturally on the Other Side.

Your soul Light is born out of what some call God. God is not a man with a beard sitting up on a throne looking down at everyone waiting to cross you off His list. Nor does He desire to throw you into a brimstone and fire like setting if you've made mistakes. God is a force that is within every soul light including the faithless and non-believers. How unconditional of Him to still love someone who makes mistakes. His love for you is bountiful and endless. He is the Light that overtakes every cell that exists in all dimensions and in all paths within and around you. When you feel and display traits aligned with love, joy and peace, then the closer you are to God. The more negative traits you experience or display, then the further away from God you are, and the less light that occupies your space. If someone is persecuting or bullying others in God's name, then you can be assured they are nowhere near God or the Light. The exception is if it is done to prevent someone from physically harming or hurting themselves, or someone else.

Higher spirit beings advise that you exhibit assertive compassion in those instances, rather than aggressive bulldozing. The latter comes from uncontrollable emotions from your ego that take flight beyond that soul's control. There is a healthy ego and a dangerous nasty ego. The darkness of ego is never at peace and thrives in the shadows by multiplying and growing. The dark side of the ego would be in a murdering terrorist, while the light side of the ego is someone that displays optimistic confidence over what they can accomplish and do in their life. Someone sure of themselves has a healthy ego, while someone slamming or criticizing someone confident and sure of themselves is operating from the darkness of ego.

There are newborn baby souls and there are the more advanced souls on Earth in a human body moving through the various stages of evolvement. Newborn souls are the student souls who immediately enter an Earthly life upon being born out of the Light. It is generally their first life run on Earth. The higher advanced souls that may seem like an old soul have been around the block so to speak. They are the teachers, inventors, leaders as well as movers and shakers. Newborn souls tend to be on the naïve side and use the most amount of malicious ego because their soul has not grown enough to effectively battle the Darkness that contaminates it. The word naïve might be too innocent of a word to the damage this soul causes, but in the eyes of the angel's *naïve* is the word they give me.

The newborn baby souls instigate the most disruption and donate the largest amounts of negative energy while contributing harmful pollutants that cause tragically damaging results on humankind and this planet. They might be the soul that spends their days criticizing others in an unhelpful way by posting malicious comments at everyone or those around them. They name call, bully, and put others down. The targets they hit can be over someone's physical appearance, or if that person does things differently than they do, or lives in a way they do not approve of, then they will attempt to assert domination over them. In the end, they are unsuccessful since the Light ultimately overpowers the darkness in the end while lifting up the bullied.

The souls that exude dark energy full time are someone you do not want to be around or spend that much time with if you can help it. They will lower your vibration and cause enormous quantities of inner or outer turmoil. They will create roadblocks that prevent you from moving forward and lead you down the wrong path often without trying to. You might be stuck living or working with someone like that. You want to steer clear of this individual since they can bring about your soul's downfall if you don't rise above it.

Not all baby souls wreak havoc on others in a negative way. There are just as many good newborn souls as there are bad. The newborn souls that are good tend to evolve and advance their souls growth at a rapid rate beyond that and into the next stratosphere. A newborn soul can also be someone without drive to accelerate or improve themselves and their soul. This is because they do not have the growth tools to do so or they do not know any better. Their soul's energy is rendered stagnant in those environments. They might be governed by their ego and doing what they were taught to do by their families, peers, and society around them. They are a product of their surroundings going through the motions of how they were trained to by others during their human developmental years. They elect to come back and have another Earthly life in order to polish up and advance their soul. Some of the newborn souls are destined for greatness, but are growing up in a setting that does not support soul growth, but rather restricts it.

If you're aware that you're not like everyone else and you feel like the outcast in your surroundings, then this is a sign that you are a gifted evolving soul waiting for the right moment to make its mark on humanity, if even to allow your soul's light to shine as brightly as the Sun on those around you. The road will eventually lead you to that place naturally on its own time.

Where a newborn soul might follow others, an advanced soul would be the leader who takes charge and goes against the crowd. They manage to rally up equal interest and opposition in the process. Advanced souls know without a doubt they are here for a larger purpose. They also understand what that objective is. There is no question or doubt about it. They might struggle in young age, but eventually will dive into their purpose at some point in their life. An advanced soul is a disciplined individual. It is someone contributing something positive towards humanity, themselves, or others in some way. The advanced soul elected to come here at this time for larger purposes they must master and accomplish. This is like a college student rising through the different levels of study along their education journey. Although in this case the evolving soul's education is connected to their continuing rapidly evolving soul growth.

CHAPTER NINE

The Soul and the Spirit

You ask an atheist where did the first human being come from and you'll get a wide variety of responses from things like you can't ask that question because it's illogical or a silly. They have said that you can't just believe you have to conclude your reasons as to why you believe based on science. You'll get a wide variety of responses that never technically answer the question. It's like when you ask a hardcore religious person where God came from or what does he look like or anything else associated with some of the extremer beliefs. They stare at you blankly or answer the question without answering it. Both extreme sides will at times also attack the person asking the question, which is another tactic to avoid answering a question you don't know the answer to. When the most acceptable answer above all that would be, "I don't really know, but it's just what I believe since nothing else has made sense enough to me to believe."

It's interesting how similar atheists are to fundamentalist religious followers in that and many other ways. This in its essence is an example of a soul consciousness choosing to make their belief system their current reality, which gets thrown out the window when their human body dies. All the nearly eight billion souls roaming the planet at this time have their own individual consciousness that is creating their current reality. This consciousness within their soul that has some measure of intelligence and the power to increase this intelligence over time is easily influenced or swayed by what it reads, what it watches, who it associates with while shunning anything or anyone else that is the anti-thesis of that. When the truer way to evolving a soul's consciousness in a greater way is seeking to understanding the fundamental compartments of the human condition and how that coincides with the soul part of that body. Even scientists have discovered they've made mistakes since they are human which equates to being infallible.

The film *Contact* was based on the book by scientist and author, Carl Sagan. What I loved about it was the interesting dichotomy between the Jodie Foster character who was an atheist scientist and her close friendship with the Matthew

McConaughey character, a Christian philosopher. For one I loved the idea they were able to be close friends despite that one area where they had extremely opposing viewpoints. You rarely hear something like that happening today between two people, even though in my personal life my friendships are across the board in belief systems and values. In the film she winds up having a questioning spiritual like experience that leads her to believe the possibility of something else out there beyond the physical human life. This propels her to come to the conclusion that she believes this to be true based on faith. Faith – a word she never thought her scientific analytical mind would ever use to describe why she believes something. As an atheist scientist her whole life was based on finding verifiable evidence until she has that one experience that knocks her solid world off kilter. In that transition on her quest for something else out there, her soul consciousness receives that awakening that transforms her to something she never thought possible.

You are a soul in a human body, but when one describes your soul's vibrational energy, then this could be talking about your overall spirit. When you are let down by a relationship connection that ends, then one might say, "This relationship broke my spirit." This is your all-inclusive life force energy, rather than the soul that inhabits your temporary vessel. It is also a metaphor because your spirit can never be broken. What they mean is that it broke your symbolic heart, not your physical heart, but your heart chakra's life force. At the same time, there have been numerous medical and scientific studies that indicate how negative feelings of any kind have a negative effect on your physical heart and health. This means feeling sadness over a breakup or death can cause cardiovascular stress. When my Spirit team and I discuss ways of helping you work on your well-being state, this also has a positive effect on your physical health. All parts of you are intertwined and connected from the soul, to the spirit, to your physical body and complete consciousness.

When you are born into an Earthly life, you're flowing with abundantly high vibrational energy that cannot be contained. This energy is your life force. As your soul moves into a human physical body, it becomes confined and suppressed to a good degree. The soul often feels suffocated dying to get out. It will seek out ways to achieve this including through unhealthy ways.

High vibrational energy is in the space your soul lives in before you enter a human physical body. This energy resides within your soul's core. It is always accessible even when you feel disconnected from it or when it's been severely lowered while travelling along your Earthly life journey. An impenetrable wall might surround it, but it is still in you deep down for access. You can either try to work on bringing that energy force out or wait until your physical human death when it bursts out of the body you inhabit and you're brought to your soul's natural state when you reach the gates of Heaven. It is wiser to work on bringing it back to its most instinctive state possible while here, rather than live a life in permanent misery. Working on improving all aspects of you has a positive benefit on your soul's consciousness and physical, spiritual, and mental well-being.

This high vibrational energy within the core part of your soul is shattered over time at the hands of the society that surrounds the newborn human child. This society is made up of your caregivers, your peers, your community, the town you live in, and the media you engage in. Those around you naively impose their often-harmful views that create an array of seemingly impossible roadblocks and hurdles for that child of God to climb out of. For some, it may be that you were born into an abusive household, or at the hands of a caregiver that viciously inflicts values in you that cause you to despise others because of their life choices or that are different from you. Hatred towards a group is often taught to you by your community, caregivers, influencers, and peers. This includes hating or disliking anyone of any race, religion, sexual orientation, political affiliation, gender, and so on. You lump them together in one group to express your disapproval of all. This is not coming from a place of Godly love. You may know someone like this, or you might even admit to yourself when you've been guilty of separating others out of anger. When your higher self is the dominate ruler of your soul, then you are more likely to correct it after realizing you've crossed the line and are not viewing circumstances clearly. There are good and bad people in every possible label created by human beings. There is no discrimination when it comes to who chooses to govern their life through the lower self or higher self.

The ego views circumstances in a perpetual hazy darkness. You may have discovered the hate filled ways of the darkness of ego simply by logging onto the Internet to see how humanity behaves. Technology is a great invention to bring others together much more rapidly than before, but it also shines a light on how humanity is at that given moment in time. When there was no Internet connection or media, then people went along with living the way they were trained to by those around them in that area. Technology, social media, and the Internet blasted the truth wide open to see that people are not as nice, caring, compassionate, and loving as one might have thought they would be. If every single human soul accepted what everyone is choosing to do without judgment, then there would be less anger and discrimination. Twitter feeds would be bathed in positivity or balanced calm objectiveness when in a disagreement. This is highly unlikely to happen while human souls remain governed by the darkness of their ego. If you disagree with someone, do you fall into your lower self by attacking them or do you step into your higher self to use assertiveness with communicating? It is not a realistic request to ask that one show love to all people, such as if a murdering terrorist is physically harming one of God's Children. It would be challenging to not be revved up to do something about that, which would fall into one of your soul's life purposes.

As a warrior of light soul, you are fighting in the

name of the Light to protect all souls that cause harm on one another. Many need to be trained how to respect others, which is why so many souls choose to incarnate on Earth throughout history to help contribute something positive that brings Light to the planet, while also improving human behavior and its existence and way of life.

When your peers continue to tell you that something is wrong with you because you're different from everybody else, then you are witnessing someone bathed in the lower energies of the darkness of ego. The ego generally has a difficult time accepting and loving those that are unlike it. The ego finds that person weird, unusual, and uncommon, while the higher self sees every soul as one. If you've been the recipient of that abuse, then it might have made you feel like an outcast, inadequate, or incompetent. You might spend your life trying to prove that you're not different in order to fit in. Or you avoid going after anything you want to do as you feel you won't be good enough and will be rejected. Your higher self is the soul part of you that is of God, therefore it knows it's worth requiring no human validation or approval from anyone. The darkness of ego views circumstances, people, and its surroundings in a limited way. It is unable to access the broader view that Heaven sees.

When one raises their consciousness, the spiritual portal begins to open and the Light pours into you. This Light shines brightly bringing the spiritual truth out. This truth is one that the dark ego has a difficult time absorbing or would prefer to keep hidden.

You have great soul power and stamina within to rise above the Darkness knowing how awesome you are. Who you are at your core is a perfect soul child of God. Pay no mind to the naysayers and negative critics around you and access this Divine source energy from within to be the best that you can be. When you have God in your house, then everything around you becomes irrelevant and trivial. Imagine what it feels like to know there is no element or trace of Darkness within that Light. Visualize this Light filling you up with pure joy, peace, and love You step into this Light and it immediately blasts away all traces of negative feeling or thought. This Light overtakes your physical body, your spirit, soul, and mind lifting you up in the process.

Have you ever had a love crush on someone? You know this crushing love feeling inside you runs deep and intensely to the degree that you never forget it throughout your life. Perhaps you were with someone who reciprocated this love, but then one day they took it away. Multiply that love crushing feeling when it felt incredible while in the throes of love. Even while multiplied by one hundred, the feeling doesn't come close to what it's like while being immersed and part of the Light.

While the spirit world terminology is often used to illustrate the separate planes, in truth it's much grander than that. Some believe the spirit world to be filled with ghostly spirits roaming around. The brighter aspects of the Light filled spirit worlds are the ultimate Utopian paradise that is an unbelievable spectacle. It mirrors the nature settings and natural wonders on Earth, but is even more vibrant, lush, and magical than the human mind could comprehend. It would have to be because why would a place full of 100% uplifting joy, love, and peace be less than the physical Earthly plane? The Earthly plane is a school set up that house's spirits of every variety in a human body. All souls on Earth are students, with a quarter of that being both student and teacher. This is because even a teacher is a student learning new things while living an Earthly life.

A spirit is also an entity, such as the entities that reside in different planes other than the Earth dimension. Spirits might appear translucent or opaque to a clairvoyant, but back home in Heaven's spirit worlds they have physical bodies. It is not the same physical body that a human body is. They appear in any shape or form they desire to morph into. The physical body they inhabit, and display cannot be harmed the way a human body can. It is in its perfect state and can shift from male to female if it pleases or into a light source or other figure.

God, the Light, and Heaven see your true nature and who your soul is. Who it is at its base is all love, peace, serenity, compassion, and joy. These are some of the highest vibrational qualities built into every soul.

A murderer's soul is seen with love. This doesn't mean they get a free pass for their wicked ways. Somewhere along their Earthly life the dark part of their ego took over and chose to do anything in its power to sabotage that soul's purpose. Their ego could have been developed and programmed into their consciousness as early as age three in human years or it could've been infected by the Darkness in the darker part of the Spirit world. When the soul exits the physical body and crosses over back home, then it is faced with choices to make that can bring the soul to redemption. Some of that entails another Earthly life in a less than stellar circumstance than their current one was. Other souls are put to work and take the long way around through the back gate of Heaven, which is a separate doorway.

There are some dark love undertones to this. Perhaps your lover's soul has become lost in purgatory, or they end up in another spirit realm and you never see them again. It's not impossible to visit them should that be the case, but from the human mind's perspective, the worst is generally feared. When you cross over, you move onto other destinies that are not always the same as someone else's, including your loved one on Earth. Still it is possible to travel and visit one another once you've crossed over. This travelling between worlds to see them happens in a matter of seconds. We take cars, trains, and planes to get to different cities on the planet, but this is the slower way compared to traveling in the spirit worlds.

Your soul is the spirit part of you that is not part of your physical human body. Your human body is a temporary vessel your soul is renting out for a limited time. When you're born into a physical human body, you enter this life through a human female. This is the beginning of one lifetime for you. This human body starts out as a physical human infant and grows up and ages over the course of a short amount of time. In Heaven, it is the opposite where one's basic appearance remains the same. On Earth, the human body is limited and for some those restrictions vary in endless ways.

Some choose to enter this life in a wheelchair, or you might have asthma issues, mental health battles, or another human physical limitation. All of this is to endure certain circumstances to overcome and accept that will have a positive benefit on your soul's evolving consciousness. When you are connected to spirit even while in a human body, then the boundaries that inhibit you from forward motion are non-existent.

You are loved beyond measure in Heaven. It doesn't matter what or whom you've chosen to live this lifetime as. Whether you are male or female, rich or poor, gay or straight, religious or atheist, and no matter what race, or political affiliation you choose, all are seen through the eyes of Heaven as being equal. The separate labels are what the dark ego of the human mind chooses in order to feel superior or separated from others, when in truth all labels are irrelevant. Using labels creates separation by viewing reality in a limited way. When you only see the love in someone else, then you're able to access the parts of that person that the angels see.

The angels see who the soul truly is when stripped of its dark ego. When you become defensive or argumentative every time someone says something, or you get upset over every news headline, then this is coming from a place of ego and your lower self. There is no truth or love while in that space. Seeing the love in others is seeing life through their eyes and understanding what their reality is like. This does not mean that you're accepting someone's bad behavior or horrible words they might have darted your way. If that's the case, then it's best to cut them out and extricate them from your vicinity. This is about taking issue with the small stuff in a profounder way that it does nothing to help anyone.

Some hang onto anger over trivial issues such as a friend having to cancel a lunch date on you since something else came up that they needed to do. It's giving someone another chance and offering forgiveness to anyone who desires to make amends with you. If someone is interested in strengthening your connection because they feel horrible about the way they behaved, then hear them out. Too often others have a wall of anger where you think the person has some nerve calling to say they're sorry now.

Holding onto anger breeds a mold like Cancer within your body that spreads like poison slowly attacking all parts of you from the physical to the spiritual. When you come from a place of love and acceptance, then the cold parts of the emotions you're feeling evaporates. This doesn't mean you have to be best friends with someone again, but hearing them out and thanking them with compassion is taking the high road. It is being diplomatic and civil with no traces of animosity in your heart. You no longer have to engage with them if you choose not to. Leaving it on a high note is operating from your higher self.

I understand the difficulties that arise when you're trying to see the love in someone else who has done wrong in your eyes. You realize the naivety or selfishness that someone else has shown and it can get under your skin. On one level it is the human ego that was bruised, because the spirit soul part of you doesn't operate from that same ego. It has an emotional detachment to everything around them.

These Divine rules are guidelines that contain a structure much like the Ten Commandments had the intention of doing at that time in history. It's to train human souls to grow, expand, be compassionate, become better people, stronger, and more evolving. In the end, none of the stresses, anger, and negativity that you experience has any bearing on anything once you've passed on and travelled back home. Suddenly whatever you were holding a grudge about will be trivial and irrelevant.

Call on your Spirit team to help you in the areas where you're having trouble forgiving someone for something erroneous. This benefits your well-being as well as everyone around you. Release toxic emotions to Heaven for transmutation.

The way you learn to see the love in others is by seeing the love in yourself. See your soul in a way that God and the angels see you. To them you are perfect in every way, even when you fall and make mistakes. When you plummet down a path of addictions, they still love you and want you to accept and love yourself enough to want to stop damaging all parts of you. There is no judgment despite what some might believe. There is no discrimination because they view you in a broader and more profound way that is difficult for a human ego to comprehend.

Your Guardian Angel is the one that lifts the pain off your heart that drives you to an addiction to cover up pain and to forget about life for a spell. Someone that operates from a lower vibration will have distaste or be repelled by someone confident and self-assured. This is considered a threat to the dark part of one's ego. Someone evolving and looking to build, enhance, and grow their soul's consciousness is attracted to someone that exudes radiant like soul confidence. They admire someone that loves and appreciates themselves and what they can produce. Pay no mind to those who attack or bully you for being sure of yourself. You are operating from a higher frequency by standing in your power and loving the totality of you. Love all that you are and shout it out from the rooftops, and from the highest mountain, because you are magnificent.

CHAPTER TEN

The Higher Self

Earthly life is tough for millions of souls. It feels like an uphill battle that never ceases. To put your soul under so much pressure that it ultimately crushes you is the kind of heaviness that Heaven wants to prevent you from experiencing. For some, it results in premature death due to the compounded stresses you've placed upon your back. No soul on Earth is exempt from that as it can affect the souls moving through all levels whether it's a newborn baby soul on up through the mid-level and to the evolving soul. All are affected in this same way by the stresses of Earthly life, including myself on up to the Dalai Lama. I mention myself, because I am forever a work in progress. Life does not have to be that hard where it kills you early in life. When you come to the realization of where this resistance is coming from, only then can you begin the process of experiencing true freedom. This freedom is what your soul craves. It longs to be released from the confined ridiculous structure that human ego has designed. Avoid falling down the path of destructive addictions or suicide to get away from the chokehold this life has on your soul.

Earthly life today has a never-ending supply of material distractions such as cell phones, computers, jobs, rents, mortgages, poor diets, toxic relationship connections, lack of exercise, stress, depression, and the list goes on and on. All these things and much more block the divinity within reach. This holiness is accessible and resides within your innate nature. You do not need to search for it or move to another area to find it. You're carrying the answers within you.

People live in big cities on top of one another and that contributes to the suffocation of your soul. Therefore, implementing soul enhancing practices when possible can assist in lightening this load and make living in nearly any condition somewhat better than manageable. When you walk through an empty park or garden, then you've noticed that you suddenly begin to feel calmer and more relaxed than you were before you went out into nature. Your mind awakens and clarity seeps in with an attempt to yank your true higher self's nature out to dominate again. There are basic ways to reach that serenity space your soul craves where you're reminded that God is with you. This also helps as a physical health stress reliever. Many avenues in which your soul can find this freedom exist on the planet in these healing nature settings.

Hatred and negativity are a poison that chokes you. Putting in an effort to display love, compassion, and fun will lift you up allowing your soul the freedom to float above the clouds. This soaring feeling is where you grow closer to God. You have pieces of Him within you, therefore you are Him. No soul is exempt from this despite what they may or may not believe.

You are perfection through the eyes of all in Heaven. The *you* that is the truest part of you is your Higher Self. Your higher self is located in a more sophisticated state of awareness within your soul. It can be obtained by rising above any negative thoughts, moods, or toxic consumptions. You reach that higher space when you are clear minded and centered. You have access to this higher self since it is the true you. The false *you* is the one that struggles against the current and falls into physical superficiality.

Put your higher self back in charge whenever you find you've been faltering into negativity. You can do this by releasing the need to manage circumstances that are beyond your control. You accept and emotionally detach from that which bothers you. Work on letting it go since it is not worth it in the larger picture. You do not need it. Invite your Spirit team into your life to guide and assist you in this process. You can do so by sending out a request to God and your Spirit team mentally, out loud, or in writing.

You can say, "Please help me." And it is in

motion.

Bringing yourself to your natural state is where you see things through the eyes of love. Your higher self requires nothing because everything is as it should be. If a mistake is made, your higher self learns from it with indifferent emotion and moves on. Your higher self efficiently corrects the mistake without drama, because it knows that all is well. This is just an Earthly life run and should not have to be so complicated. It becomes complex when you are mired down heavily in physical desires and functions taught to you by society. You have to get a job and go to work to make money to physically survive here. It's understood that this is how physical Earthly life is. You can still go after the physical necessities you require without getting obsessively bogged down in it that it stresses you out or makes you permanently unhappy.

To move into your higher self's state is to not desire or want. What you want may not be aligned with your higher self's state. You may want someone specific in your life in a love relationship, but this person is not someone that will be on an equal footing as you. Heaven sees someone else on its way into your life that is aligned and around the same level as you spiritually. This is why most souls attract in those who are similar to them to a degree. When there are vast differences in vibration to someone else, then the connection grows challenging and sometimes breaks apart. Exceptions are balanced Teacher-Student relationships where there is a compassionate give and take.

Your vibration is moving up and down throughout each day depending on what is being thrown at you. This is why it can be difficult at times to be in your true self's state every second on this turbulent planet. Your day starts out fantastic and you are in your higher self's state. You are happy and full of love. You get in your car and someone cuts you off or honks their horn. You suddenly feel stress and agitation. This gradually moves you into your lower self's state. That is until you bring yourself back up to that space of feeling centered and at peace again.

It becomes a juggling act or a yo-yo as you learn how to adjust your frequencies throughout any given day. You might say, "This would be easier if I didn't have to deal with people." But this is not necessarily true. You could spend all day at home alone and not doing much. Soon you reach moments where you feel unmotivated, lonely, isolated, secluded, depressed, or bored. Those states gradually begin to lower your vibration into your lower self's state. No one caused it, but the negative thoughts in your mind. This is one of the challenges of living an Earthly life.

A pioneer conquers new territory by being themselves and going against what the masses believe in order to promote positive change. Think for yourself even if you stand alone. Stick to your guns even if others disagree or attempt to bully or attack you. It is more than likely that you will be bullied and attacked at some point in your life if you haven't already. The dark ego is threatened by those that are strong, different, rebellious, outspoken, or a know it all. Pay no mind and stay focused on your life purpose and goals. Someone may confront you at some point in your life. Lower vibration human souls are threaded out among those who operate on a higher level. The lower evolved is threatened by someone that rules at life. Ignore that kind of energy as it's irrelevant. You have a job to do, so refuse to back down or fill yourself up with fear that you will not be popular by going against what is expected of you.

For some, the idea of an afterlife is a fairy tale that gives one hope for those that fear death. This is a false belief conjured up by those that do not experience day-to-day connections with source. They might have never reached that one defining moment in their life that convinces them enough that there is more beyond their physical existence. The more in tune you are, the more you are likely to have profound experiences with the spirit world that perk up your ears.

It is difficult now more than ever in history for a human soul to connect with something beyond. They are distracted by the physical demands of Earth from buildings, cars, phones, computers, electronics, drama, violence, negativity, and noise. The list of blocks between humankind and Heaven are endless. This has led souls to grow up on Earth not believing in anything spiritual related. To believe that there is a God that sits on a throne above the clouds casting judgment and waiting to punish man is the real fairytale, but God is another name for all that is. Every cell, every atom, and organism that exists is God. He is everywhere filling up all available space possible in every plane, realm, universe, and dimension. You cannot run from Him.

There are some that do not believe in an afterlife. They have come to this conclusion due to a strict religious upbringing that was filled with negativity and judgment. Or they might not believe in Heaven because life has dealt them a poor hand. They might end up being confined to a wheelchair and they look at that as a negative. Often those situations are a result of accelerated spiritual growth needed. When one finds that at some point in their life that a major handicap or challenge has taken place, then it's intended that you begin to view the world and all that is around you in a broader or different way. The goal is to awaken your mind if it was previously closed. The other case is the handicap came upon someone because the physical body is not infallible. It will be met with challenges that evaporate when you head back home to Heaven.

An atheist will protest to not believe there is another place one goes to when they pass on. They believe that when you die it's the end. Although some profess to be atheists, they are more agnostic when they reveal statements aligned with the belief that your mind is open enough to allow room for the possibility of there being some form of God or afterlife. This is pending they can receive concrete material-based evidence on that; otherwise the conclusion is that it must not be true since they've never seen it. The evidence will not show up in a math equation. The data exists when you fine-tune all your psychic senses. You open them up a crack to receive a divinely guided message convincing enough to your ego that ultimately helps you ask the bigger questions and notice the possibilities of more being out there.

I have been testing my Spirit team and Heaven out my entire life. I do this because I don't blindly follow or believe in something I cannot see. I have an analytical mind and require some measure of proof that convinces me, so I understand skepticism. I've had repeated occurrences where I've stated something that was about to happen, and it later has. Everyone has that connection and at one time or another may be able to recall those instances where they've noticed this same psychic phenomenon.

The ego cuts off the communication between the non-believer and what exists outside of them. Your ego is what sabotages you and tells you that you're not qualified and have no business doing anything you want to do. Your ego's voice instills fear and causes your life to feel chaotic, while the higher self's voice is filled with overflowing love, calm, or excitement. Your ego's voice changes its mind daily and often, while your higher self's voice is stable, faithful, and frequent. Your higher self's voice will continue to push you to do the same thing repeatedly for years until you finally do it. That voice would never urge you to do something that would ultimately bring you or someone else down. There is a domino effect to your decision-making process. When this happens, it is a clue that your choices were made from the ego.

Your ego pushes you to act in ways that cause pain, hurt, or confusion, while your higher self's voice gives you brilliant flashes of ideas that never leave your mind. When you implement them into action, then you experience success, love, and joy. The ego will make you feel as if you're bouncing around, stagnant, heading nowhere fast, or going around in circles and never accomplishing anything. While your higher self pushes you to make changes that benefit you and others. It might coax you for decades to finally write that book, make that video, and apply for that job. While your ego will delay you from moving forward and will say you're not qualified to write a book. It'll tell you that you don't have the time, or it will instruct you to wait until you're more settled. When you listen to that voice, you can be assured that you will never accomplish anything, and nor will you ever write that book.

You hear those who are of older age express regret, "I should've done this or that. It was always on my mind too, but I never did it." Right there is a clue to the heavenly guidance you were receiving most of your life, but you ignored it. Those listening to their higher self's voice are suddenly filled with glorious love and excitement. Pay attention to what's going on inside you in order to decipher what is your higher self and what is your lower self. Examine the repercussions, challenges, or blessings that come out of that as a result of your action or inaction.

CHAPTER ELEVEN

Soul Growth Through Grief

The next two chapters we'll look at some of the harder soul challenges for people. These are connected to experiences such as grief or battling an illness. These sorts of challenges have made people question if there is a God, angels, or anybody that cares. How could a loving God create so much suffering? I've suffered on every level possible throughout my life that could make anyone question their faith. A great deal of suffering is caused by humankind. Either we are generating the suffering ourselves or another person's free will actions have generated the suffering on us. Some want a guarantee of a pain free life, but that doesn't exist on Earth while living a human existence. The pain free life exists when you head back home to Heaven.

We come to Earth to teach others lessons and learn lessons from others as well as through our human experiences. While some may have a hard time believing this, Earth is a school for human souls. When you head to a human school like High School or College, no one promises that it will be easy. You will go through highs and lows as you are learning something in these higher institutions. The same goes for the soul that lives an Earthly life. You will be tested by yourself and by others. All of this influences your soul's consciousness. Grieving or battling an illness have their own array of challenges with it that benefit the soul's consciousness as difficult as that might be to consider.

Grief is part of the human experience. It can be the sadness over the death of someone close to you, but it can also be grieving over the loss of anything of value to your soul such as the loss of a pet, a job, an apartment or home. It might be the loss of a friend or love relationship that ended. It can be losing anyone or anything that means a great deal to you. Perhaps someone you loved moved away from you physically, mentally, emotionally, or spiritually. It can be a friend that moves away to another state or country. Even though you remain in touch, it's not the same because you're not physically hanging out in person absorbing one another's energies. The energy is more potent in person than it is through the technological waves.

Grief can be present over the loss of a job or the hurt over something valuable to you. The grieving feelings one experiences with anything are the same bereaving emotion across the spectrum regardless of the circumstance. It still brings on the same pain and despair.

Offering Supportive Strength for the Grieving

Being a supportive friend to someone grieving over any loss or a physical death of a loved one can require delicate understanding. It is your role at that moment to step into the teacher role by being there for that person. You might wrestle with whether you should get into the spiritual talk by discussing how the soul never dies. That truth can be too far-fetched for someone to think about after they've lost someone. Deep down they may understand and already know it to be true, but it will not matter at the time they are battling with that major change in their life. Everything the one grieving usually believes is temporarily tossed out the window, because the feelings they have for the person that is no longer in front of them is so powerful. Grieving is a part of the soul's growth and experience. It must be allowed to freely feel whatever they sense in that moment without restriction or blockage.

When you're battling the depths of grief there is nothing one can truly say to you except to be there for you, to be present when needed, give space when you know the one grieving wants to be left alone. This doesn't mean vanish and disappear, but instead be within arm's reach and accessible by periodically checking in with them. Reminding them they are not alone and that you are there.

Perhaps you're a friend who is the practical joker or the funny one who never gets that emotional. This humor part of you is a gift to the grieving that needs some relief from the pain if only for a short time. They might ask to hang out with you for the purpose of forgetting about the grief for an hour or for the day. They know you're the fun one or the jokester that is exceptional at getting everyone to forget about any stresses, sadness, or troubles. This helps in keeping their vibration high while teaching them how to laugh again.

Others grieving may want that friend who is the deep insightful one. They crave your philosophical nature. While others may want the whole gamut of friends from the funny one on Saturday, then the insightful deep one on Sunday. Some want the variety of friend experiences in order to feel the entire spectrum of emotions and understandings when it comes to the loss of someone dear.

Contrary to my work being on the more serious side, in person I'm more of the practical joker coupled with the philosophical insights and guidance. I've had friends going through tough grieving times in the past. When that's happened, they've reached out to me that they need me to help them forget. They've spent so much time with others showering sympathy and condolences, but they need that no-nonsense fun time to relieve their soul of the pain.

Depending on how attached you were to the person that physically left, you will experience grief over it. The grieving emotions are still the same regardless if the person passed on in human death or physically left the relationship you had with them. It still feels like something was ripped out of you leaving your soul to suffocate. You feel like you cannot breathe or continue with life. You become depressed and bed ridden feeling like you want to die. Reaching for a toxic addiction doesn't help, as you feel even more miserable afterwards. There is nothing anyone can say that can make those feelings disappear. It is the soul's individual experience to move through on their time frame.

As a supportive friend, the best you can do is be there when the grieving wants to talk, or if they want someone there in the room with them where no talking is required or necessary. They feel a comfort knowing someone else is in the house, even if you're both doing your own things in different rooms. Sometimes the grieving wants to be distracted from the feelings. They know that you can get their mind off it just by being yourself and who you typically are.

Don't beat yourself up if you're doing everything you possibly can to make them forget about it and you find it's not working. You're making them laugh, or showing them a good time, yet you look over and the person experiencing grief seems to be somewhere else and completely distracted and down. Don't take that personally because it has nothing to do with what you're doing or not doing. You are helping them even if you're not realizing it in that moment. You're already a comfort by being there. They will appreciate that if not in the moment, but long after they've moved past the grief.

The last thing you do not want to say is something along the lines of, "You need to move on."

This shows you feel put out that your friend is not in the same happy content space that you are. Feeling put out is not a genuine friend.

When you're grieving, then it becomes about you and what you've lost, and how will you go on. You will not want to go on, as it's too painful to get up every day and put on the face that all is well, when deep down you're still in pain.

Little by little and gradually as time moves on, the wounds will heal and close, even if the scar is forever present. You will become stronger than before viewing life in a broader way through this tumultuous emotional experience. It can help you realize what's important in life. Earthly life goes beyond your job that helps pay the bills, or the material desires you continuously chase after. Suddenly everything on Earth seems trivial after you've gone through a grieving experience.

You never want to shove your personal doctrine or belief system to someone you suspect doesn't share your beliefs or is not ready to hear it. This is regardless if it's a grieving person or not. The exception is if they ask you for that wisdom or for your view on the death.

There are many things you can do to support someone grieving over the death of a loved one, and that is to be a friend. Let them know you're there if they ever want to talk. Unless asked, don't get into the whole soul never dies speech if they don't believe in it or if they're not in the right state of mind to hear it. When someone is upset and feeling grief, then anything you say will not be heard much anyway.

Grieving Through a Tough Circumstance

Grieving is a state all soul's experience at one time or another when a loved one has passed away or moved on from them. It's part of the cycle of human physical life. Spirit understands that you have every good reason to be distracted when a death happens, and they will never stop communicating with you regardless. They will never stop working with you to heal your heart and help you continue. They will work to put signs in your path that the person you lost is still around you even if you're not physically seeing them. If it's the loss of a friend, relationship, or job, then they'll work with you to help you see the loss as the beginning of something better for you. There are millions of stories over the centuries where someone admits to noticing that their deceased loved one was communicating with them at one point.

The human experience part of you produces heavy grief at times. Sad emotions create a block with the Divine cutting off all communication. It prevents you from hearing them making it seem as if everything has gone quiet. Spirit is communicating with you especially during the grieving process, even if you're no longer picking up on anything. There is no time limit to healing as each soul has their timeline where the healing happens naturally on its own. There are positive blessings in motion outside of what seems like a tragedy and it is beauty in its simplicity.

It can be painful when someone you care about passes on, let alone when it seems they've left too soon. You worry if they've left peacefully, which is the ego creating those fears, since souls exit this plane peacefully and smoothly. It is the human existence part of you that brings in a tidal wave of grief. There is no time limit as you move through it since this process can take as long as your soul needs it to.

A Death Welcomes a New Beginning

A death can be the death of someone close to you, but it can also be a metaphorical death where it's the end of one way of life and the beginning of a new chapter.

Heart related issues are the leading cause of death in humankind. My spirit doesn't see human death in the way that others do. It's not that I don't feel it because I do if it was someone close, but I don't view practical human circumstances in the same way that others might and tend to. I've been viewing it through the lens of my Spirit team, which is less emotional, but sympathetic and empathetic to the pain someone is experiencing. Depending on my state of mind that day, my perception can vacillate between Spirit's eyes, then my ego's eyes, to my higher self's view, then the lower self's, and back around again. It swings all over the place like a pendulum creating a vast reservoir of emotion inside.

The morning my father passed away, the paramedics, the firemen, and the policemen that were present had all approached me in a group like a mob. One of them said, "Can we talk to you? You seem to be the only one together here."

That remark stood out because I hadn't given it much thought until I realized that everyone seemed to notice. It was only when they said that did I scan my surroundings realizing how upset everyone was. They added that I appeared to be standing in a calm centered focused state. I've had film producer friends all say at different times over the years, "You're like the calm within the storm."

You say the word "Death" to humankind, and it's viewed with darkness. You conduct a web search of the word *death* and you receive pages of dark images or the grim reaper. This is the perception humankind has of death to the point that those images are #1 on the web search engines, because more people clicked on those images. There is no soul death, even though the soul's experiences are met with endings and beginnings. The soul moves on and begins a new chapter, but any death is not a tragedy. It simply means your current life run is complete. Your soul evolves out of this existence and continues on to a place that is much more magnificent than Earth, but mirrors that utopian ideal your soul longs for while here. Death shouldn't be dark or negative, and I've had death throughout my life on all levels.

CHAPTER TWELVE

Soul Growth Through Health Issues

Mental health issues affect millions of people around the world. The general list includes depression, anxiety, and the various ailments from eating disorders, to psychotic and mood disorders. Those suffering from some form of mental health issues find that it prevents them from living the kind of life they dream of. It can prevent you from going after what you want or inhibit you from defending yourself. For some it can lead to suicide or permanent stagnancy.

Depression sufferers feel inadequate or unable to motivate themselves to live. Agoraphobics are afraid to leave their homes, or they feel uncomfortable in crowded or confined spaces. Those with social anxiety avoid accepting invitations to parties or functions, as they fear being watched, judged, or simply cannot handle the huge number of psychic stimuli tampering their emotional sensitive system. As you get to know others on a personal level, there isn't anyone who isn't battling some form of disorder or phobia connected to one's mental health, especially in this hyper technology age that has been shown to have aggravated it. You might never fully diminish the disorders in one lifetime, but you can get close to where you're able to function somewhat realistically in this hostile world and form some semblance of a life.

Almost everyone on the planet has some sort of neurosis, while others may battle harder versions of these disorders. Some of these disorders are genetic and inherited. They run right down the genetic blood line. Other times it's taught or placed on the back of that soul. Many struggle with disorders their entire life or attempt to temper it and keep it under control.

For those that battle disorders, it might please you to know that some of the most successful people in the world battle some of these same issues. Entertainers from well-known actors and singers wrestle with social anxiety. They can train themselves to shut it off temporarily when they are in the performing zone, whether on stage or in front of the camera. This is one of the positives of diving into creative pursuits whether professionally or as a side hobby. Some are born into this life with a mental health disorder, while others develop it over the duration of their Earthly life due to human societal tampering.

Due to the rise of technology, selfies, and phones, narcissism is a trait that is grown and bred into the generations raised post 2000. From that point forward, Earth's history moved into a generation being raised on technology, selfies, and computers. This has rendered many incapable of carrying in person conversations or exuding proper class etiquette. Many are growing up in environments where they are assaulted by selfishness in others every second. You cannot hide from it or be unaware of it unless you live in the middle of nowhere or never go online. This along with poor diet and nutrition all contribute to the high amounts of anxiety, depression, and mental health issues that exist.

Some choose to take anti-depressants or anti-anxiety medication, while others refuse to as they feel that it alters their brain chemistry artificially. They prefer to engage in counseling with a therapist or talk therapy instead, while others participate in counseling along with medication. These are choices that are up to you and your doctor. It's your life and you and your doctor know what's best for you to get through it. Ironically, I've discovered those that are against medication that may need it seem to self-medicate in other ways that are not exactly healthy.

As someone plagued with social anxiety my entire life, I understand what's it like to wrestle with it. Those suffering from social anxiety know what it's like to have their thoughts, feelings, and heart racing for no apparent reason. Someone is walking towards you to talk to you, and you want to jump out of your skin. You want them to go away. You don't want to have to talk to them, deal with people, stand up, and give a speech, and so forth. You desire a daily pill to keep those issues contained as much as possible. Do what you feel is best for you. There is nothing wrong with wanting to be on medication or wanting to dissolve medication. This is a personal choice that you make. With anything health related, always seek out a professional medical doctor regardless of what anyone states. Take hold of the reigns and govern your life the way you see fit. What's important is that you're addressing any issues you're battling with in a healthy way.

All mental health issues go away when the soul crosses over. Until then you learn to adjust your lifestyle and way of living to help it be more manageable. This is the same way anyone who suffers from any form of mental disorder this lifetime. If you have social anxiety, then you don't spend your days heading to areas that are jam packed with people. If you go to an amusement park, then you go on a day that you know isn't so crowded. You avoid going to the grocery store at high noon on a weekend when it's typically more packed than at any other hour.

You might be driven to mask the mental health issues through toxins that make you wish you could stop. Efficient ways of eliminating a toxic addiction such as bad foods, drugs, alcohol, cigarettes, caffeine, or coffee is by gradually reducing it over time.

I understand the day to day struggles that exist in life as I've been through those trenches too. I know how to navigate through it. I've been in the gutters of addiction as I have an addictive personality, but I also have a strong connection with the Other Side. I've learned from Heaven that the only person beating up on you is you. Everyone has their own gauge on what works for them. It's about doing the best you can. If you fall off the wagon, you don't beat yourself up. You get back on the horse again and continue moving forward one day at a time.

Hyper focus on anything expands whatever the attention is on. If it's focused on a health concern, the healing takes longer to come about. Great health improvements are made through prayer and by shifting your focus positively away from the issue. I've had catastrophic health issues that were painful, but went away after I believed it would improve and get better. Instead I focused on fun, joy, laughter, and did whatever I could to get to that place from watching a funny movie to joking around with a pal.

There are shattering health issues that do or will come about that are beyond human and Heaven's control. It's better to look upon it with positive thoughts rather than negative ones. The negative thoughts will only make you feel that much worse. At least the positive thoughts will ensure you remain in high spirits throughout the process.

I've had major health scares in the past that were

physically painful, but I continued to ask for Divine help and eventually one day it was no more. It was as if it never happened. I have days where I'm not focused or my faith is waning, but I quickly revert to being focused not long afterwards.

When you work on taking care of yourself regularly and treat what you put into your body with the utmost care, then any illnesses that arise are minimal. This doesn't mean you'll be problem free, but it can help in making it less tough. I've certainly felt worn down as if I was coming down with something, but as soon as I'm aware of that, I immediately up my preventatives before it blows up. I wake up the next day feeling great again. When I feel my body under stress and my immune system declining, I'm guided to begin my remedies to get better quickly. I immediately double the water and vitamin C intake. I sleep earlier and longer than usual while avoiding strenuous exercise or anything that can cause anxiety. I may do wheatgrass and blue algae shots as well as making sure I'm relaxed and detached from any stress. This is partially why I haven't had the major flu since the early 2000's, knock on wood.

Exceptions to this are you may be an older person or younger unhealthy person where it takes longer for your body to fight off illnesses. There are also circumstances where you discover it was beyond your control. You may be born this lifetime with a weaker immune system you have to battle, so you do the best you can one day at a time. Surround yourself with supportive people that can give you what you need.

When you feel a cold or the flu coming on, immediately start the medicinal regimen. Drink lots of water and up the Vitamin C intake. You can go as far as to drink a shot or two of wheatgrass if you can keep it down. Above all sleep more than you usually do. When your body is wearing down, this is a sign that you need to take it easy and rest. If you watch movies, then stick to comedies, since lightheartedness, joy, and laughter raise your vibration. When you're sick or your immune system is crashing, then your vibration is low. This will help raise it and help you get better quicker. Avoid strenuous exercises during this time so as not to wear your body out and dehydrate it. Although some exercise is helpful such as casual biking or walking, but you won't do that when you have the full-blown flu.

Drink more water than usual by doubling it. If you drink fifty ounces a day, then aim for a hundred ounces spread out through the day. Head to bed earlier than you normally would. Sleep, water, and prayer will rejuvenate your body quickly.

Other preventatives might include water with squeezed lemon or lime, and a dash of cayenne pepper. Add a healthy sweetener, or agave syrup if it's too difficult to take down. Heat it up and then sip carefully. Other flu and cold illness fighting preventatives that are high in Vitamin C are jalapeno peppers, onions, algae, and garlic.

You can call on Jesus or Raphael. Archangel Raphael is the healing angel to call on for all things healing, health, nutrition, exercise, and well-being related.

CHAPTER THIRTEEN

Soul Growth Through Relationships

Now that you've made it through the wilderness of grief and illnesses, let's move into one of my favorite subjects to discuss. Love and relationships! One of the bigger benefits towards the soul's evolving consciousness is through your relationship connections with other people. The lessons while in those connections is invaluable. In the spiritual arena we call these connections soul mates, so we'll continue to use that label for the sake of understanding.

Every soul on the planet has many soul mates. They can come in the form of friendships, family members, colleagues, and love partners. Some of these relationship dynamics are considered karmic relationships, soul mate connections, and the rarest of them all the twin flame. It doesn't matter what you choose to label or call it, because the intention and meanings of each are evident. Every soul on the planet has or will experience numerous karmic and soul mate relationships. As challenging as it might be to accept, the soul knows the family they will be born into on Earth. When you say that to most people the initial response is, "Boy, did I choose wrong." The more tempestuous and antagonistic the family connection, then the more lessons learned. The more lessons learned, the quicker the soul consciousness evolving process is. You don't grow much residing in a picture-perfect palace where nothing happens. The more tempestuous a connection is, then the more likely it is a karmic connection. Your soul mate connections are the ones with people that push your buttons and push you out of your comfort zone. They have endless roles with some of them being sent to act as catalysts to help guide you from one area of your life to another.

Twin flame connections are a rare relationship dynamic because most of the time one's twin flame is back home in Heaven's spirit world. There is little reason for a twin flame to be on Earth at the same time as their twin flame. Why would they when you spend an eternity with your twin flame back home. One of the reasons they would incarnate relatively at the same time would be for the sake of helping one another's accelerated soul consciousness growth and evolving process, or to be a supportive partner in some way that benefits one another's fight to improve humanity through humanitarian efforts and work. It is typically the soul's that have moved into the post graduate higher evolving end of consciousness when they are more likely to meet their twin flame this lifetime. This isn't with every single higher evolving soul, since many choose to live single lives while focusing on their larger purposes. They understand they came here for that larger purpose that takes precedence over anything else. The main goal for twin flames is to act as support the way any teammate supports one another on the sports field.

It would be nearly impossible to attract in a quality mate for life if you are wrecked with low self-esteem or if you're battling any kind of turmoil or addictions. This is especially the case when it comes to the twin flame connection, because both partners have reached a relatively balanced alignment between one another spiritually and emotionally. This doesn't mean it is without issues that either individual battles with, and nor is it about the occasional turmoil, wrestling of addictions, or low self-esteem one has from time to time. This is about the soul that fights a daily uphill battle of struggle that endures for years.

When I was battling all these issues and more up through my twenties, the partners I was bringing into my world were battling similar circumstances. In hindsight, it was too obvious not to notice the pattern. While in the throes of battle, you'll attract in an undesirable situation or partner, or a rebound soul mate catalyst to move you out of the sphere of soul consciousness you're currently in. This is someone sent to you for the particular purpose of assisting you in moving past turmoil, drama, or addictions. Their soul's job is to inspire you to improve, but that doesn't necessarily mean they're the long-term friendship or love partner. Once their job is complete, usually those types of connections begin to dissolve and then an even more together friendship or love partner shows up. The in-between soul mate partnership is taking you from one point to the next where you then leave and encounter the greater partner that follows.

The catalyst soul mate partner is to work in tandem with you to heal something from the past. This might be where two people connect and discover they are battling the exact same issue of getting over a love relationship break up or a job loss. Because of their mutual understanding of what it's like going through the same thing, they can relate and work out the issues together in conversation by this common denominator. The connection that is forming is no accident.

The friendship suddenly feels like two best friends hitting the road together, but often once the core issue is worked out and both are over the loss they experienced, they notice that their connection starts to wane or grow tired. It may drag on a bit longer than usual until one day they realize they're not connecting the way they used to. This is because the job they each had as soul mates for one another has been complete. That job was to get you both from one station to the next. There may be some cases where you know it's over and begin distancing yourself, but the other hasn't reached that level of realization and is holding on for dear life.

You cannot wait around for this catalyst soul mate partner to show up to help lift you out of turmoil and bring you to the next station on your soul's journey. When you're waiting for a rescuer to pull you out of your life, you could be waiting indefinitely. If your life is stuck on pause due to circumstances or past choices, and there is no soul mate catalyst coming in, then lean on God to lift you up. You can do this by requesting His intervention and help through regular prayer. Make prayer a regular part of your daily life if it isn't already. Have faith and believe you are being helped even if the effects are not visible. You also must do the work and stand strong in faith to make the necessary efforts, adjustments, and action steps to improving your life one day at a time, which simultaneously contributes to raising your consciousness.

Examine where your overall self-esteem is at because a low self-esteem will not attract in a healthy life, let alone assist in the soul's evolving process. It only invites in more issues. A low self-esteem person may be constantly comparing themselves to others, which is not hard today for so many people with access to social media. Everyone is comparing themselves to others and feeling less than in the process. A low self-esteem person is more likely to become abusive with a friendship or love partner by lashing out at them. High self-esteem people are not bullying or attacking others in any way. There's no reason for them to because they are sure of who they are. The low self-esteem person may attack through backhanded ways where they make fun of someone not realizing they're doing that to prop themselves up. They break others down so they can be falsely lifted. If the partner on the receiving end has high self-esteem, then they will eventually walk away from the connection, because those types of partners are not interested in abusive situations. Even though you may not have realized you were behaving that way until after the relationship has dismantled and you fall back into the low self-esteem traits again.

A sign that someone is evolving their soul is they grow surer of themselves and confident. They are not comparing themselves to others the way they might have done. This is because when you evolve spiritually, then you're becoming more connected to what is beyond the triviality and superficiality of the physical world. It's no longer of interest to you to resort to petty comparisons.

What are the traits you love about yourself? What are traits you cannot stand about yourself? What are the areas you can change to adjust the parts of you that make you hate yourself? What are the areas that you can't stand about yourself, but you know you cannot change?

Feeling truly whole is loving all that you are. It is accepting all parts of you especially the uncomfortable parts. It is raising your self-esteem into a warrior like confidence that you are content being alone and independent. This is not to be confused with being lonely. Loneliness and being comfortable alone are two different scenarios.

Warrior like confidence means you are also in a perfect space of peace. Only when you love yourself in this grand way can you be more than ready for the greatness that matches that kind of vibration. You will have the occasional low periods in life as everyone does. It's human nature to experience ups and downs. You might feel the random low self-esteem hit or you'll feel tender about the way you look or certain parts of your personality. This is about your overall state and demeanor, not the occasional stresses and lows that everyone can feel from time to time. It doesn't mean you have to beat yourself up attempting to be consistent about it, because that would be an outlandish and unrealistic request. You're human and you have human emotions that are generated and connected to the ego, which in turn tampers with your feelings and thoughts.

We all vacillate from the positive to the negative every day. To demand that someone be positive around the clock is an impossible unrealistic demand. This is about finding a healthy balance to being fully aware of the range of vibrational energy you're radiating throughout each day. This is all part of the process of evolving your soul's consciousness. As you move through the different levels of evolving, which include all the challenges and pitfalls in life, then you come out of it with a newfound sense of serenity and outlook. This is when the most ideal partner will move into position in front of you.

CHAPTER FOURTEEN

Twin Flame Soul Mission and Purpose

When a soul chooses to incarnate into another Earthly life run, it is because they have a purpose, goal, and mission to doing so. This mission is a solo one that will entail numerous purposes within them. If the soul is rapidly evolving their consciousness, then the likelihood of connecting with a twin flame partnership are great. Like karmic and soul mate relationships, a twin flame soul can be a friendship, family member, business partner or lover. The twin flame would only incarnate at relatively the same time that enables both partners to simultaneously encourage one another's higher purposes and goals in offering that person support in some manner and vice versa.

The twin flames are like a spark of fire. When fire burns up the land and terrain on one end, and there is another fire burning separately on the other end, then depending on the direction its headed, those two fires will eventually connect and merge. The results are combustible! It can create a power that is beyond human comprehension burning everything in its wake. When two twin flames connect on Earth, this same metaphor set up takes place.

Both twin flames already have a commanding presence that is sensed by others when they enter the room alone. When that same person walks in the room with their twin flame, everyone notices and feels it. The energy is incredibly passionate and deep that it is beyond ignorable. It's what it truly means to say, "Those two over there are a power couple." They almost look like the same person, even if they physically look different. It is the similar intense energies that people are picking up on.

Twin flames tend to be go-getters with enormous goals and missions and purposes to accomplish throughout their life that includes improving the state of humanity by being who they are and the work they set out to do. Someone that is idle, lazy, or has a slacker mentality in general will not be meeting or encountering their twin flame. Because the twin flame is not needed since the person is not contributing anything positive towards the betterment of humanity on any level whether through teaching, or the arts, or humanitarian and charity works, etc. There is something about each twin flame person that is identifiable and unusual beyond any physical attraction chemistry.

When your twin flame is in the spirit world, they may work as one of your guides to bring soul mate connections into your life. They don't want you spending your days longing for love or companionship, so they assist in the process of bringing you potential lovers, friendships, colleagues, or acquaintances for soul mate connections.

The reality is also that not everyone will experience a romantic love partnership, let alone one that lasts until the end of their days. This leads to the myth that there is someone out there for everyone, which is a misguided romantic notion that doesn't ring true for every single person on the planet. It's also a fictitious assumption to feed the masses with, especially when it is not realistic or practical. There are millions of people that will never obtain a love partner or are not looking for one.

Usually a sudden love feeling experienced on Earth comes from one's Spirit Guide, Guardian Angel, or Twin Flame on the Other Side working with them. Some people are without friends, family, or lovers. This doesn't mean that Spirit has ignored them. Potential soul mate relationships are brought to all souls, but that doesn't mean they're making the connection happen and keeping them alive. Someone can get you a job interview, but it's up to you to get the job.

Numerous soul mate potentials cross paths with you, but it's up to the both of you to say hello and build a connection. No one in Heaven can make that part happen. You're not a puppet on strings. You are a thinking, feeling, conscious person who has free will choice to create the life you desire. You have free will choice to take that Divine sign given to you and act on it or disregard it. You might recall positive blessing circumstances that could have happened in your life, but you unknowingly let it pass on by. It was only later in hindsight when you looked back that you wish you could have acted on it.

Some people choose to live a loner hermit lifestyle away from other people. They have free will choice and they have chosen to live this kind of life for various reasons. Sometimes it's due to circumstances that led them there. For others, they might be highly sensitive, divinely connected, agoraphobic, and therefore unable to withstand the nonsensical erratic energy that is typically being emitted off many people. The loner has chosen this life and is not necessarily looking to increase their opportunities of crossing paths with soul mates.

Technology and social media give you instant ways of connecting with others. This has made it easier for souls to interconnect if only via a computer or phone. If twin flames find each other online, then they will eventually find a way to be close to one another physically at some point during their lives. They both have a deep desire for this because to not do so is indefinitely crushing.

They need to be in the same vicinity of one another and will do whatever they need to in order to make it happen.

Embarking on an Earthly Mission

The twin flame is the ultimate deep love that transcends all. Most twin flames are on the Other Side and not living an Earthly life. One of the common reasons all souls incarnate into an Earthly life is for the purpose of teaching and learning. The twin flames are together on the Other Side for all eternity, so there is little reason for both to incarnate into an Earthly life, unless there is a larger reason, purpose, goal, and mission to do so. This would be one that requires the both of your Divine powers to work in tandem. They are one another's champion in all aspects of their life.

Earthly life is a blip on the radar, a millisecond on the clock, compared to soul eternity. This is one of the reasons why not all twin flames incarnate at the same time. One of the twin flames decides to incarnate into an Earthly life for purposes laid out in its soul contract. This is before heading back home to Heaven when their mission is complete. It is back home when they are re-united with their twin flame who has been watching and guiding them on their Earthly journey along with their Spirit team.

If a mission is incredibly greater than the norm, a twin flame may incarnate not long before or after its soul partner to offer support and receive that similar support in return for a spell. They become a powerful duo when they're together. There is no telling what they can accomplish while united on Earth. Both are brought to one another to evolve their mutual soul consciousness together.

Mirroring, Repelling, and Attracting

The twin flame soul connections repel as much as they love each other, but this is predominately in the beginning. Usually one or the other is about to embark on a major spiritual transformation where they soon rapidly begin to evolve their mutual souls' consciousness. Twin flame relationships may break up, get back together, break up again and get back together. This is not the same as relationships that operate in the vortex of high drama or ones that have constant arguments, which is a Karmic connection. Twin flames have an endless calm love for one another even when splitting apart. There is little to no emotional blackmail, arguing, or drama between them. If they split apart then they will eventually coast right back into each other's arms or lives again.

There is a point where they stop splitting up and stay together permanently for the rest of their current Earthly lives. This has been more so the case post-technological modern-day time, since the choices one has on the planet are not as limited as they once were. Twin flames can find one another much easier today than they were eons ago. Even though they can find one another easier, it is still not without its challenges preventing them from coming together right away.

The twin flame partnership has pain and confusion in both partners while they're apart, but it's not their intention to cause this pain. The aloofness causes hurt enough. They are always telepathically connected, even if they're not together physically. When they re-unite, they will often bring up synchronistic circumstances where they were both thinking or feeling the same thing as the other one was.

If one of them feels as if the partner is up to no good, then the other partner is likely feeling the same way in return. When they sit down to talk about it, they realize they're both thinking and feeling the same thing about the other one. They also discover that what was assumed in both is unfounded. They must learn to trust one another and ensure that trust is proven and reciprocated. The twin flames effortlessly communicate telepathically while on Earth. This is due to both evolving rapidly in one lifetime that their senses grow even sharper while with each other. There will never be a case where one is in tune and the other is not. Both seem to display similar behavior patterns that it is almost like looking in a mirror.

Back home the twin flames have faith and trust running between them naturally, but on Earth they are tempted by Earthly physical material egotistical pleasures that can cause break ups. This is also another reason why the twin flames rarely incarnate at the same time, because when they do they have evolved and transcended high enough that they are not typically tempted by the Earthly pleasures and addictions that tend to break apart connections or stall forward soul movement. They are not immune to addictions, but it is on the rare side if the temptations are severe enough. They are more likely to display the temptations and addictions earlier in life, but by the time they move into the thirties and above, they have worked to minimize, reduce, or eliminate that way of life and thinking.

While one of the partners, typically the older one has evolved quickly, the younger one shows signs of this evolvement, but is still wrestling with releasing the temptations on Earth that wreak havoc on the lives of human soul relationships. They are still operating from egotistical desires that may have more to do with human genetics, such as an alcoholic gene passed on from a parent.

Twin flames may likely be from different backgrounds or towns on the planet. They might have an age gap of six to ten years or more give or take. The reason is because there are more lessons to gain with someone that comes from a different background or cultural influence. Both of the humanitarian and spiritual part of their nature tends to explode in larger ways when they finally merge together. Both partners continue to gradually evolve beyond that while in the confines of the relationship that doesn't feel like imprisonment at all, but true freedom since they also operate independently. While some people feel suffocated in a love relationship, the twin flames feel alive and free when with one another than while single. This is also the case even if one or the both had generally observed non-committal traits in their dating life and previous relationships. In one sense, they were subconsciously waiting for their right soul mate, which they truly never felt they had in previous partners, even though they enjoyed whoever they were seeing at the time while in the moment. This same essence between them is also evident if the twin flame connection is a friendship, family member, or business partner.

The twin flame connection defies all this uniting them naturally and effortlessly. There is no effort because when they end up in the same room together it is like magnet and steel colliding. It will happen for the most non-committal person on the planet. The union pushes both partners to evolve even more while in the presence of one another's spirit lights. It is while in the relationship together that whatever spiritual plateau they had reached before that moment, the connection takes them higher than that and in ways they didn't know were possible.

Twin flames tend to be leaders that are quite independent due to their spiritual evolving process. Souls that are rapidly evolving are less interested in functioning in groups, while being more comfortable alone or as a leader of sorts. They also tend to show little signs of co-dependency, while revealing exceptional leadership skills due to being comfortable with who they are.

From a soul level, when the twin flames re-unite this lifetime, it equally excites, inspires, and ignites the other's soul to greater heights neither would have reached without the presence of the other.

This inspiration continues until the end of both of their Earthly lives when they re-unite back home.

Twin flames do not join just to unite to make love on a beach for the rest of their life. There is a purpose and reason the two have come together on Earth that is beyond the core basis and desire for having a love relationship. It is all connected to evolving their soul's consciousness.

Usually the twin flame will show up just before the initial mate is about to embark on another spiritual awakening or transformation change, while the other may be years behind them. If this is the case, the younger in Earth years twin flame may accelerate their spiritual evolvement while with the older one, or the connection will temporarily break apart. This would be the case due to the younger one not being emotionally ready for an intense connection. They may be of different human ages, but they are the same soul age.

At the same time, they cannot stand to be away from their twin flame partner because it feels like a hole is missing within them. It never goes away even if they end up with other people. Twin flames are like a triple header soul mate connection that compliments one another to climb enormous altitudes. It's like the Lunar Eclipse displaying the power of three Full Moons on one day. Soul mate connections can be intense, but the force of a soul mate connection can exist on various levels from the physical to the spiritual. Whereas a twin flame connection is primarily on a spiritual soul level first and foremost beyond anything else. The partners see one another's soul behind their eyes regardless of what they look like. They can be a couple that is intensely drawn to one another for decades, but purely on a platonic level. Their sexual nature with one another may be somewhat non-existent for human physical or emotional reasons, yet they cannot be apart from one another.

The twin flame connections are not always love related, which on the one hand may be a blessing for some. If the two incarnate relatively at the same time during one lifetime and fall in love, it will be more intense than if your twin flame was a best friend, family member, or a business partner you've joined forces with for life.

Those around that witness a twin flame connection when they are together will point out the natural ease they notice both have as if they are made for each other. They might point out that until their friend met this person, they were unstable or floundering all over the place, but now that they're with this person they've never seen them thrive and improve so dramatically. They will point out that they both seem to have the same essence, movements, and moods to one degree or another. And others may point out that they seem like they even look the same, even if they are physically different in appearance. There is something about the cosmic kismet like feeling that shows them to be two peas in a pod. Once together on Earth, they never leave one another's side even during splits, which seem permanent, but often the splits end up being temporary.

God splits the soul in two to give each soul an eternal partner, but the twin flames will decide how and when they will choose to be together. To be with someone for eternity is a long time, so both souls will have periods of their existence when they're not with each other.

CHAPTER FIFTEEN

*Soul Growth Through
Work and Career*

The jobs you have in life all contribute to the evolving process of your soul's consciousness. You might think you're stuck in a dead-end menial job, but there is something you are gaining there beyond a paycheck. One should do their best to be grateful they have a job in a world that has become increasingly difficult to find work for so many people. If you hate your job, then I'm sure that anyone that's been unemployed for years would be happy to take your job off your hands. Volunteer work and charities also count as work that is affecting your soul's consciousness.

We're often thrown into testy situations with

other people where we are having to learn lessons like patience in getting along with a personality that is opposing to you. One of the greater wishes by many is to find work that has meaning to them. Often jobs that have a great deeper meaning to you are connected to one of your life's purposes. When you put joy into your work, then this raises your soul vibration in the process.

Working in a job or career that has deep meaning and fulfillment to you while getting paid for it is something many want to achieve. It can be frustrating when you're an intelligent thinking talented consciousness who has dreams of wanting to partake in work that means something to you, while being efficiently compensated enough to survive. You find you're stuck in a life soul crushing job that you head off to day after day simply for the paycheck.

Career transitions are challenging for anyone, because transitions in general are life altering and require effort. Many self-employed entrepreneur success stories also discuss how difficult it can be at first. I've always been a huge fan of rags to riches success stories since I was a kid. Those are the stories that reveal someone who came from nothing and made something out of their life. They weren't born into money and nor did they have a well to do life. Instead they had to work harder than those who were born into money or had stuff handed to them. They had the struggles where it seemed impossible, but they soon climbed the ranks to the top. Those are the inspiring stories that remind you that anyone can do it if they believe and try hard enough.

This isn't necessarily about accumulating financial riches, which is a hollow superficial goal. This is about being able to turn your life purpose, hobby, or passion into a career where you are making enough money that you no longer have to work at jobs you despise just for the paycheck.

Rags to riches stories often entail someone that just wanted to be able to do work that was their passion. They weren't looking to make a million dollars. The financial abundance that came flowing in was a positive side effect to them putting effort into their passion. They put in positive energy that came in naturally because they were enjoying the work. This attracted in the financial abundance.

When you feel no guidance or messages coming in from above, then it could be that you're experiencing a psychic block. Therefore, raising your vibration is an important factor to consider, because doing that assists the evolving process of the soul consciousness while helping to dissolve any blocks that give you a stronger Divine connection. Everyone is born with psychic abilities that never go away even if it feels that way. Those gifts vary in frequency from one to the next. The psychic senses are hanging out under the surface and always accessible. When you don't feel psychic, it just means something is blocking it. Blocks can be certain toxic foods, drinks, negative moods, bad energy, technological distractions, and other people to name a few. The closer you are to the physical Earth such as in nature, then the easier your abilities can begin the process of being reawakened. The physical Earth is anything that is not manmade, such as buildings and cars. Certain lifestyle changes need to be incorporated into your life as well such as stripping yourself of potential blocks. One way to raise your vibration is through exercise and working out. This assists you in being a clearer vessel with the Divine, not to mention the health benefits you receive out of that too.

I've forever been a strong advocate for exercise since I was a kid. Since my teen years, I've been into exercise, working out, and taking care of myself as much as possible. I'll go hiking in the mountains, to rock climbing in the desert, to regular jogs and biking on the beach where I'll hang out for hours connecting with Spirit. This is because exercise awakens every cell in your body and soul, but so does being in nature. When you're exercising in nature, then that's a double whammy that assists in raising your vibration. Those cells that are awakened are transporters that communicate with spirit beings from beyond. When those cells awaken, then the information flows in more effortlessly. Exercise does a body good releasing happy endorphin chemicals. Happiness lifts your vibration cracking open the Divine communication line.

Getting into a happy state, exercising, and being in nature will all help raise your vibration. When you combine all three at once, then what a powerhouse feeling that is. A raised vibration is what acts as a funnel for your Spirit team to communicate with you much more easily. It also brings in free flowing good stuff into your world.

Forcing happiness or pretending to be happy won't work, so it will have to be authentic joy. Exercise has always been like oxygen to me. The initial getting to the exercise may be tough for some, but once you get into some form of cardio to get the body warmed up, then this gets the oxygen working through your cells. It feels like soaring above the clouds making you feel good.

Display Optimism and Gratitude

It took me a long time to move away from relying on regular day jobs to pay me and realize the income was ultimately coming from God. You could do your life purpose work if the financial support part of it is given to God to pay you. You develop less worry and guilt, and more faith and optimism knowing that you're taken care of when you modify your thinking process. This is by changing your perspective to understand that God is ultimately your source of income. This is rather than heavily focusing on a company or a boss to rely on to stay afloat and be taken care of. It takes a great leap of faith to be able to let go of that control. Jobs come and go, but God is always constant. All forms of abundance are trickling down from God, to the company, and to you. It's no accident that you're at a job. You are gaining important soul lessons through all your human experiences from your job or career to your relationship connections.

If fear or worry enters your mind, then alter

the sentence to something positive: "Thank you so much for your help with this. Thank you for the blessings you've bestowed on me to date. Thank you also for ensuring I have a place to live without fear or worry that my bills won't get paid. Thank you for my strong health and happiness."

A huge lift inside can be felt when changing your sentences from something challenging and negative to something aligned with gratitude, optimism, and faith. When you heavily complain about things never going your way, then this creates a huge heavy burden on your soul while bringing more of that into your life.

Worry creates more worry, while joy creates more joy. When you feel like your job is not going as planned or you hate it, and your mind constantly goes there whenever you have a free minute, then take a step back and halt the tone of that thinking. Shift those words to ones of gratitude. Look at the reasons behind why you might be required by spirit to be at that job during the time you are. Think of the good things you have in your life. The ones that would make your life worse if you didn't have those good things. They can be items such as your car that is in good condition helping you get to and from work without worry. You don't worry much about your car until something goes wrong with it, then you realize how grateful you are to have a car that runs. Don't wait for something bad to happen to realize what you have, but be grateful now.

It's easy to take things for granted until those blessings unacknowledged are taken away. When you are in a negative space, then stop and direct your attention to the blessings you currently have. Maybe you've reached the point of feeling sorry for yourself. You find that you say things like, "Why does everyone else get the good stuff, but I'm still struggling to get my share of the blessings?"

The same ones feeling sorry for themselves regularly will also moan about not having any friends. When you look closer, you notice they seem to be surrounded by numerous people that fit the description of a friend. They're still unhappy and despondent not seeing it because perhaps they have conditions on what they expect from a friend. You can have a pity party begging for attention from others, or you can get over it and continue persevering on doing what you're called to do. Never beg for anyone's friendship and attention. One often looks at what they don't have, rather than what they currently do. Pay attention to the blessings existing in your present moment. Acknowledging and displaying gratitude for what you have now is a positive abundance attractor.

CHAPTER SIXTEEN

Soul Growth Through Superficiality

P art of raising your soul's consciousness includes having a higher view of Earthly life. Getting bogged down in superficiality can create a block due to the delusions it casts upon your soul. Current human life today has propelled others to become obsessed by youth and exterior appearances. For some it is to the point where reality has fazed those that have fallen into the epicenter of this superficiality. There was a time pre-technology when you respected your elders. Now many disrespect those older because they are ageist and under the delusion, they are untouchable and exempt from aging. What is failed to realize is they will age and be discriminated against as well, unless they are lucky enough to reach older age when the upcoming generations of souls have moved out of that shallowness. Otherwise, they will have a much harder time with ageing because of this inability to accept spiritual reality early on. It is unlikely that any immediate generations will rise above this kind of showiness due to how prevalent and saturated exterior looks have dominated the Internet waves.

There was the infamous case between the years of 1585 and 1609 when Hungarian noblewoman *Countess Elizabeth Bathory de Ecsed* allegedly had hundreds of virgin girls tortured and murdered. This was to be able to bath in their blood. She believed bathing in the blood of virgins would help her retain youth. Cut to hundreds of years later when Earthly life moved into modern technological times in the 1980's, 1990's, 2000's and beyond. Popular culture in Entertainment became more about visual appearances in the music industry, rather than making and playing great music. Magazines airbrushed their models and celebrities almost to the point of making them unrecognizable in some cases. Even the most amateur photographer on the planet who enjoys taking their daily selfies will ensure that the filters are just right. The photos must appear attractive enough to post for validation and praise. There have also been endless cases of people getting killed or falling off a cliff by trying to take that perfect selfie or shot to gain more likes and followers. Chasing numbers that become irrelevant and obsolete when you exit this plane.

This all stems from the ego part of the soul's core desire of longing to be loved, admired, and praised. Some desire praise and attention more than others to the degree of extremism. A soul was born out of love and will die right back into that love. It moves about in a human body longing to be hugged, cuddled, and loved up. When that love is starved from their existence, they may harden and toughen up, become distant, aloof, and indifferent. Or they may head in the opposite direction and compensate by trying anything and everything to find ways to gain that praise and admiration that never sticks. Any validation lasts for a millisecond until they notice that people have moved onto other things and no longer have any interest in them again. It's dangerous to place your well-being state in the hands of others. Relying on people online and around you to continuously prop you up and feel good about yourself can become tiresome from all aspects. Love yourself and all that you are now.

The body is temporary and aging every second until it stops working and disintegrates. This scares some causing them to be unsure of what happens after that. They may believe there is life after death or they're hesitant because they don't see it with their own eyes. The one thing everyone agrees on is that we will all cease to live on this planet forever. Those that invested deeply into the physical material world may have the greatest fear involved. The reality check will hit them on their deathbed when the material and physical fades away.

As you grow older and your soul consciousness evolves, then this can help some in becoming more fearless when it comes to death because you know it's coming. You reach the realization that you don't have a choice and you must find a way to strengthen your faith and resolve. This is partially why you may have noticed that as one grows older their spiritual belief system seems to become stronger. This is the case even if they were a non-believer in younger age. Perhaps they won't suddenly believe in God, but they will grow more open minded of the possibilities of something good beyond their Earthly life. They subconsciously know that their body will permanently stop working for good. It will shut down and become lifeless. They may hopefully see that their soul consciousness is somewhere in there and that it will continue on.

The human bodies were not designed to live forever. You reach older age signified by your physical body aging and eventually shutting down. The body will die, and the soul will exit and move on to new destinies. There is no way around that. No one would want to live on this planet forever since back home is where the true fun and serenity exists full time. You are with those in your soul tribe, whereas on Earth you are mixed in with all souls in various levels of growth. Many of those souls use enormous amounts of dark ego, which dominates over their higher self. This is what causes so much unrest and unhappiness on the planet.

During the dawn of the first human civilization,

people were living to be hundreds of years old because diseases were rare, diets weren't tampered with the way they are now, and stresses were low. All of that changed and transformed as human beings began to decide how people should live. They designed and created a life that has ended up creating more stress. They started to mess with foods and diets in a way that has slowly killed people off early. Diseases, health issues, and plagues were bred as a result. The average human being was passing on in their age thirties. This has been reversed to one degree where lives have been extended significantly by the healthier choices many make. People are also having access to better medical resources that didn't exist centuries ago. The ever growing and expanding spiritual metaphysical movement has been helping to make one another's souls more aware, conscious, and enlightened about life beyond the physical and superficial.

At the same time, many are passing on early due to heart related issues, which is connected to the stress filled lives that many live. When it becomes all about making money and working for the sake of working, this puts on stress, especially if you're not doing work that is done out of love, or for the sheer passion and enjoyment of it. Some are working with people that are irritating or stressful on a regular basis, which has a negative toxic affect. They infiltrate that onto others with the intention of crushing that person's life force and well-being state. Energy expands and flows around you and it will hit all those in your line of fire regardless if it's good or bad.

God and the Angels are egoless, which means they're not bothered or affected by the damage humankind causes on one another. This isn't to say they don't have a conscious. They have the biggest consciousness that exists. They're not emotionally affected by anything the way human ego is. There are beings in the spirit world that have an ego, but it is not the dark ego that plagues humankind. These are the spirit guides, saints, beings from realm worlds, and departed loved ones. They are affected and bothered by humanities treatment of one another, but not to the degree that a human being might be. They don't have the same ego that human beings have because their ego is highly evolved, aware, and in check. They'll view it the way an activist might when reading terrible news about something being taken away from another person. It's observed with an emotional detachment

Heaven has never been terribly pleased with the direction and state the planet has gone down no matter what period of history it's in, yet they are aware there are many spirit beings all over the planet doing their part to contribute something positive towards humanity that is aligned with love. These souls incarnated on the planet to contribute to the betterment of life on Earth. The goal of spirit is to bring all into a higher evolving consciousness and vibrational state possible, so that Heaven can exist on Earth. It will take centuries to reach that state if at all. You can see this as being the case if you examine the barbaric nature of human beings throughout history. That toxic monster nature is still present on the planet, but instead of nailing people to a cross or violently killing them, the toxicity resides and expresses itself through other people's feelings and thoughts through a technological device.

There is goodness threaded out amidst the darkness of the world. The good deeds taking place are enacted without the desire for anything in return. Because it's seemingly rare, when it does happen, you're floored and prompted to take a step back in stunned amazement.

The love available from above never ceases all throughout any personal ordeal. This is also to help face the soul in the direction of this source of love. It's only hoped the soul can snap back into the true higher consciousness to realize that none of the drama around them matters, and nor is it based in reality. You've given your power away to a ruler or a group thinking they have jurisdiction to help you feel better.

Those good well-being feelings you're attempting to access are built into you available for accessibility. You don't need a group to prop you up in the end. Maybe you did in the beginning as you wore the training armor to get your feet wet and to help you grow strong, but in the end, it was never needed.

You might show love to the Universe, your guides, your team, God, and all in Heaven, but it's not because they are soaking up the love you return tenfold. They have no ego and have no desire for those elements because that love is already built into them. The love essence is their true nature, so they don't desire something they already have. Those same love elements are also a part of every soul on Earth, even though it might seem as if someone has strayed far away from it through poor actions, behavior, or cruel words. Heaven is so busy loving that they are impartial to whether you love them back.

Reaching that moment of awareness and awakening is one of the greatest gifts you can give your soul. You become that much closer to transcending utopia. A personal awakening of the soul consciousness is like the rapture where the trumpet blows, and the sky parts, and the Archangel descends with a shout! This is the moment when light is shed onto your consciousness and you see things you hadn't noticed before. The answer was always there, but it was as if you were previously living in darkness. It's a beautiful incredible feeling reaching that state of knowingness. The truth was always in front of you, but you hadn't paid much attention to it until that moment of awareness that feels like a magnificent exhilarated release. Only then are you taking your first baby steps into utopia.

CHAPTER SEVENTEEN

*Soul Growth Through
Emotional Healing*

When seeking to convey optimistic positivity, it cannot be a forced fake positivity since that energy is picked up on as negative. It's like putting a Band-Aid over a cut. The cut is still there as an open wound, but hidden underneath the Band-Aid. Your fake positivity is the cut covered by a Band-Aid. The Universe and Heaven know your general state even if you try and fake it. You cannot get away with a lie or hide anything from any being in Heaven. They all know what you are hiding underneath the essence of that energy. What you do, say, feel, or think is in plain view to them. This is the case even if your actions are different than how or what you feel or think.

Sometimes you can be putting on the happy face, when deep down you're miserable. You may not even be conscious of doing that. If you realize you have been conveying a fake positivity where you show the world your optimism, but deep down you're hurting or in mental or emotional pain, then that is the first step towards spiritual recovery. You've admitted you're battling while putting on that smile to others.

If someone you were in love with rejected or left you, then it is absurd to assume you're going to bounce back an hour after they left and dive right back into life like it never happened, unless you are a gifted sociopath with no emotions. You're going to feel the gamut of challenging feelings that may last one week, or it could last one year. For some it may be even longer than that depending on how attached to the person you were. I've witnessed cases where someone never truly bounces back after that. They are forever shaped and molded a different way than they had started out due to the traumatic experience.

You would understandably experience upset, hurt, and sadness over something like that. You are unable to pull through and want to stay in bed all day. Even when you push yourself to get outside and continue to live, you experience the kind of pain that feels as if something important was ripped out of you.

To shift that wide discord, you move through the many emotional stages one experiences with something like that. Take your time, allow yourself to process it, and make sense of what's happened. Move through the various stages of grief in your own personal way that ranges from depression and sadness, to anger and rage. You'll hopefully talk about it with a friend, a counselor, or anyone that will listen. You can also write your feelings down in a word document, journal, or an email to yourself and file it away. This is to help get it out of you. Eventually you move out of those challenging emotions as you take your time processing each one.

The healing process concludes when you can move past those negative feeling emotions and into a state where you are willing and ready to accept and release the person that has hurt you. When you release that person, then you do it with love. Meaning there is no additional pain or malice in your heart for them. You're not condoning any bad behavior they might have done, but you are kicking out any pain that attached itself to you out of your vicinity. You no longer need it. Abuse done to you is not your fault. If you instigated something, then apologize to the person and forgive yourself for the ill will you might have caused, then release it and let it go. You don't want to carry that pain around indefinitely.

Work on getting yourself into that place where you will positively be better off without that person that caused you pain. You mentally thank them for the experience, "I bless you on your path." And then you release it and let it go.

There is no time limit as to how long it can take when it comes to moving through a healing process. This can be healing over anything, such as any kind of hurt or upset in your life, regardless of what it is. For some people it can take weeks or months, and others it may take years. There are cases where some get stuck in that cycle of hurt that lasts indefinitely for years and sometimes decades if not treated or healed. The tragedy with the latter is they remain in the exact same space they were when the initial upset happened. Sometimes you may not even be aware that you're still stuck in a cycle due to something from the past.

An example might be someone who was married for decades, then an affair breaks up the marriage. This is followed by Divorce and all the stresses that come out of that. The person cheated on might carry the cheater in their aura until they release it. It is understandable that one would be upset by this kind of abrupt life circumstance that throws you a hard-right punch, but you don't want to let it stay with you for too long. The longer it stays with you, then the longer it becomes a part of you. It has the danger of shaping you into someone you might not want to become.

Where it gets exceptionally tricky is when the pain endures for years. The person never quite bounces back into life again. They just go through the motions numbed to everyone and everything around them. They become inaccessible for the right new partner or circumstance to come into their life. It also blocks the flow of abundance from coming in.

I understand this well having been through that in personal experiences. Years in I've hardened and become more difficult to get close to. Through my connections with God, I begin to see it all unravel before me. I receive that high awareness I hadn't noticed before. I mentally went back into time to try and find out when I changed or was changing. Nine times out of ten, I wound up tracing it back to some kind of traumatic experience, such as a love relationship break up or childhood abuse.

In the past, I've discussed the importance of taking those moments throughout your life to do a thorough life review. This has so many benefits that include going backwards into time to make note of the significant life circumstances that took place in your life, whether good or bad. Make note of what transpired out of that. How it might have changed you for better or worse. The worst is not about judging you. It's making amends for what changed certain traits that you're not particularly fond of, but you don't know how to change it. Acknowledging it is an important step towards changing it. You cannot change something you're unaware of.

Many years have passed after you emotionally shut down following a traumatic event, crises, or break up. You may one day awaken to realize that you had been stagnant for so long and are not sure why. This is because the incident that kicked that off was so long ago by that point, but your overall nature, personality, and demeanor had permanently changed to who you've become today. It's only when you stop to ponder and re-trace your steps backwards when you realize that who you are today was kicked off by traumatic events years prior. You had long forgotten about it, but it had also shifted your behavior patterns in the process to who you've become now. This is that moment of awakening and clarity or as some say, "A-ha! Wow, I can't believe how drastically that situation changed me. I need to do something about this today!"

The process of positive change begins at that moment you gained clarity and awareness.

You've admitted there's a problem rumbling within you. What a fantastic awareness level to reach and achieve for your soul's consciousness. Because now you can begin the steps to work on healing those open wounds that caused you to deny your feelings and prevented you from moving forward and onward with life. You want to attract in a positive abundant feeling, but you wrestle with that due to the hard life circumstances that have thrown you one curve ball after another.

Heal emotional wounds through awareness, putting in the daily work, and bringing in a counselor, healer, or therapist if you're able to. If that's not feasible for any reason such as financial, seek out groups online that share your difficulties. Having camaraderie support or others to talk to that are going through a similar circumstance has more of a positive than challenging effect. The positive effect is this can empower the both of you to stand tall and into your own. It produces healing in a quicker way than if you didn't have that support.

The challenging side can be if neither party are interested in healing and just want to rehash past circumstances for months and years longer than necessary that it turns into gossip and vengeful thoughts. This leaves you stuck in that dark state. If you've sought out help, then that means you've already surpassed the first step of being aware that you are wrestling with something difficult. Deep down you want it to stop and are ready for help. You begin the process of seeking out that assistance. You have the intention and desire to do what you can to help you through a negative chapter in your life.

I personally turn to prayer for assistance and intervention when healing is needed. Ask God and your Spirit team to work through you and to help you heal and guide you towards steps on how to do that. Request that you be helped to understand what it is you need, and to assist you in taking notice of when He is helping. Ask that He help you understand by putting that assistance in your path.

There are times that God and spirit are putting helpful signs in front of you, but when you're wallowing in a negative state you might not notice it, since a negative state can block Divine communication. Fear not since He is always with you and will continue to put that help in front of you indefinitely until you notice it. You will wake up one day and get that bright idea that puts you into action mode. When the answer appears, it feels like it had always been there, but you hadn't noticed it until that moment.

Your emotional healing may leave a scar the way a deep cut on your body can. The wound is healed enough that it makes you whole again. "Whole again" is the perfect exceptional state you were in upon birth.

I've talked to people who have massive anger issues. They admit it's caused a ton of problems in their life, but they cannot control it. Admitting you have a problem is one of the best first steps you can take that will adjust your soul and body down the path of beautiful magnificent recovery. What an amazing gift that is to be blessed with knowingness.

Have it in your mind that you want to do the work in order to make your peace with any ill will you might have caused another person or what someone else might have caused you. This is regardless if it was you causing pain for another person or you were just cruel to yourself.

You can be cruel to yourself through self-hate by your actions, thoughts, words, and feelings. You can be cruel to yourself with the addictions and toxins you continuously put into your body knowing it can result in harm. You can be cruel to yourself by saying yes to things that deep down don't feel right to you. Learning to tell others no is also a purpose some need to learn this lifetime. Naturally, there are circumstances where you do have to suck it up and say yes, such as if it is a part of your job you get paid for. This isn't about that, but about the things that morally and spiritually affect you in a negative way where you can truly say no. Your boss needs you to fax something, well of course you do that. A friend keeps asking you to do something you're uncomfortable with. Saying no to that is not being rude or unaccommodating. Saying no is saying yes to you.

This illustration is mentioned because it influences your overall well-being as well as the process of positive manifestation and abundance attracting. If you remain in a negative cycle, then this will leave your soul's life trajectory on pause for as long as it takes before you begin moving out of that state.

This applies to whatever upsetting traumatic circumstance has taken place in your life. You want to work on moving through those emotional changes associated with the experience while eventually reaching a place where you can release it. This isn't just to benefit you, your body, mind, and soul, but it also assists in helping you to continue living this life you've been blessed with. Bad experiences happen on some level for everyone, even the most seemingly privileged person. No one is exempt from enduring some form of rock and roll in their life.

Experiences both good and bad are designed to teach you lessons that positively affect your soul's growth process. The higher level your soul reaches, the greater the abundant attraction quotient is. Abundance being about your overall state of mind, rather than financial increase. The desire for riches is a hollow goal that does not fulfill in the end. Having enough income coming in can certainly bring you less stress in your life to one extent. This is in the ways that it would allow you to quit a soul crushing day job and dive into work that is your passion and life purpose. The income gained should be used to continue improving your soul while giving you more time and energy to apply towards your passionate soul driven life purpose work that helps others.

You may be perfectly content today, even though you might have endured traumatic experiences earlier in life, such as in childhood, but if you have not made your peace with what happened to you in an earlier part of your life, then you are subconsciously carrying that around with you even if you've suppressed it. This also influences your manifestation process today.

If you're attempting to examine your life today to see what could be blocking the positive flow of abundance and none is evident, then move further back into time to see what wounds have yet to be healed. Sometimes journaling, writing about it, or talking about it can help get it out of you to make your peace with it. Another additional way is to find a comfortable spot in a nature setting or a private space at home to commune with God regularly. Even though you can conduct prayer anywhere you like from walking to your car, sitting in traffic, or while you're getting ready for the day. The benefit of finding a space to have an in-depth prayer session is that it helps you be distraction free in order to fully focus on any guidance that is coming in. Ask Heaven what needs to be healed in your life. This can include old forgotten wounds that are still present in your subconscious. This will help increase the flow of positive abundance energy.

CHAPTER EIGHTEEN

The Human Influences on the Soul Consciousness

You are a conscious, thinking, feeling, soul light born out of love and having a physical human experience. At the beginning of your Earthly life, you were born profoundly psychic and in tune to all that is around you. This is the natural state of your soul since its conception. You basked in the traits of love, joy, and peace full time while in it. This is your true soul's essence. Whenever you stray outside of that you are no longer aligned with God or higher-level Spirit beings in Heaven. Instead, the Darkness has infiltrated your aura and your ego has risen and taken over your soul's true essence.

You were born with an ego that expands as it enters the Earth's atmosphere. This ego causes you to struggle and have conflicts as it attempts to take over you and dominate your actions, thoughts, and feelings. When your ego runs recklessly it grows and expands into darkness. The dark ego is what prompts you to wrestle with challenges in this lifetime. It is also what causes all the chaos, violence, hatred, and havoc on Earth.

These challenges you struggle with were called sin during ancient times, even though some circles continue to keep the word alive. In the modern-day world, the word sin is best understood as challenges. The sins committed can delay you on your path and wreak havoc on your soul's innate system. This innate system is the higher self part of you that governs your life through a broader perspective.

The seven deadly sins were created in order to assist human souls in making sounder choices. As time progressed, these sins were soon viewed as extreme depending on who was executing them. This eventually tainted the deadly sins into something evil. They were disregarded and not taken seriously except in smaller religious based circles. Although the seven deadly sins have underlying religious based tones, they are challenges that all human souls wrestle with to one degree or another regardless of religion. When you're deeply absorbed in toxic challenges, then it causes an array of issues and complications on your life path. These sins or challenges prevent the positive flow of energy and abundance in your life. They also play a hand at creating a block that stops up the communication line with your Spirit team.

As you grew from infant into childhood, the peers, community, and society around you played a major hand at your developmental process. They implemented belief systems and values that although might have been brought to you without malice, they often ultimately erected blocks on your soul's path. It's stalled the soul's consciousness from evolving, as well as dimmed the communication line with Heaven. As a result, you might have questioned the existence of anything outside of yourself because you stopped picking up any signs of your Spirit teams' guidance and messages. You can tell if this is the case or not by going back into time and remembering how you were raised and what those around you were like.

How much of your values and ways of living today are similar to what your caregivers and peers were like growing up? If they are on par and similar, then this is an example of how you were heavily influenced by those around you. If you're a Christian, Buddhist, or Muslim, and so we're most of those around you growing up, then this is another sign of being influenced by your surroundings. You adopted the way of life you were taught by those in your vicinity. This doesn't necessarily mean it's a bad thing. It's pointing out how human behavior is influenced by its surroundings. You're examining how your values and beliefs today have been heavily influenced by those around you. This continues into adulthood as you adopt new values and beliefs that your new social circles follow.

If you're in love with a potential political ruler or

candidate, odds may be that your peers have the same love. If it's not a candidate, then it's a political party. Some will stand firm on their personal moral rule that they cannot be friends with anyone who does not share their beliefs or values. They might deny this and emphatically ensure they love all, but this turns out to not be the case when an isolated circumstance pushes them to reconsider their tolerance level. This is especially the case where religion and politics are concerned. Two topics that should never be discussed at a dinner gathering or at work. Those with differing opinions cannot be convinced to see it your way and vice versa. The irony is you learn more lessons from those that have little to nothing in common from you.

You can be friends with those who have diverse political or religious beliefs from yourself, and still be able to remain close because you have other elements outside of that which bring you together. You naturally don't get into conversations on topics where you know it is opposing of one another. And when you do discuss it, you are respectful of one another's beliefs. You are coming at it from an emotionally detached intellectual perspective. This is a sign that your soul consciousness is accelerating.

Someone who came into this lifetime as a homosexual can be friends with someone who grew up Christian in this lifetime. This is as long as the Christian has no issues with their friend who is gay and vice versa. It would be debatable on how close of a friend two people are if a big part of them is rejected by their friend.

Christians receive a bad knock because the media has focused heavily on the ones that claim that being homosexual is a sin. The real sin are those absolved in the seven deadly sins, which include Pride (judgment) and Wrath (hate). Heaven has taught me over the years that there is nothing sinful about two souls coming together in love, regardless of their human physical gender. Human souls have free will choice to believe what they want to believe, even if it's not based in reality.

There are a great many wonderful loving Christians who love all souls without conditions, as long as the soul is not hurting anyone. You rarely hear about them because the media finds anything connected to goodness to be too boring for a story or worth talking about. The ego is driven by fear, which is easy to create on this planet.

The world witnesses someone preaching hate, but then you investigate how that person was raised only to discover that this person's caregivers and surroundings were like that as well too. There are cases where someone's values are erroneously distinctive. You were raised in a positively joyful home with suitable values, but you dart off in the opposite direction into a life of hate or negativity. Every human soul being is a complex character with a mixture of attributes that come in from various sources. The best parts of a human soul are the ones that are a part of God. The worst parts are where the ego has been led astray.

CHAPTER NINETEEN

*Spirit Guides
and Guardian Angels*

As we bring this to a close, let's take a look at a key factor that can help in continuing to evolve your soul consciousness. Every soul on the planet without exception has psychic senses that enable them to connect with their own Spirit team of guardians that work to guide you on your path. In order to easily access God and evolve your soul's consciousness and life purpose, He gives each soul at least one main Spirit Guide and one Guardian Angel to assist and guide where needed throughout your Earthly life. Communicating with your Guide and Angel is communicating with God. They are His hands and arms, so you are communicating with Him. Your Guide and Angel are with you from your human birth until your human death. Before you are born into an Earthly life, you commune with your Spirit team that consists of one Guide and one Angel.

It's your Guardian Angel that will be there for you during the moments when emotional healing is needed. Your Spirit Guide works with you on the practical survival stuff. For instance, your upset about a breakup that happened or the death of a loved one, then your angel comes to your side. You're having trouble finding a job, a new apartment/home, or relationship, then your Spirit Guide would help with that. It's not that cut and dry, since they both work overtime on guiding you over little day to day things too, but this is what their roles tend to be like.

A person's Guardian Angel and Spirit Guide are always near the person they're assigned to in many ways on varying levels. Being connected to them is like having a best friend in another dimension. Like God, these are beings that know everything about you, all the good and the bad. They know your thoughts and feelings, the things you hide, the things you reveal, and yet they never leave your side. They also continue to love you unconditionally no matter how horrific a human crime you've done, which isn't saying that you won't need to pay for that crime depending on the severity. This is the same love God has for all of his Children of souls.

One of their jobs is to support and guide you towards and down the right path that helps in fulfilling the terms of your soul contract. This includes through paying for karma created as well too. When you act out and cause trouble in school, then you're sent to the Principles office to be disciplined. The soul class works in a similar way, but some of the soul crimes are not all the same as the Earthly crimes. If you're headed towards danger, then they do their best to stop you or steer you away from that. Therefore, it's important to be clear minded and to develop a strong connection with them. It helps you decipher between a good decision and a bad one when you're tuned in to them daily.

Guides communicate through your psychic clair senses. There are psychic clair *(clear)* channel senses within every soul, but there are four primary clairs. They are Clairvoyance *(clear seeing)*, Clairsentience *(clear feeling)*, Clairaudience *(clear hearing)* and Claircognizance *(clear knowing)*. These clairs are the psychic channel sense frequencies in which you communicate with God or any spirit soul being in Heaven.

You were intended to have a strong connection and communication line with Heaven, so that you don't have to go through this life alone. You don't have to always figure it out for yourself when you have this Spirit team waiting in the wings 24/7 wherever you are. Your psychic gifts are not a gift at all as its part of who you are. It is already built into the core part of your soul.

Your core Spirit team are of the many that greet you as you enter the gates of Heaven. They are your team who works with you guiding you away from harm and down the path that benefits your higher self. In a sense, they do their best to help you along your life's path. This can be to assist you in picking out a school or trade course aligned with your purpose, or to finding a job, an apartment, or potential love interest that will be beneficial for you. They help with the small details in your life that you may be oblivious too.

One of the other reasons your guardians are with you is in order to assist you in accomplishing the varying purposes you agreed upon prior to entering an Earthly life. They are also present in orchestrating situations that will be benefit to your soul's growth.

If you are someone with a strong connection with the Other Side, you pray to God regularly, you're going through tough human life experiences, or have a purpose that is beneficial to the betterment of humanity and this planet, then you likely have more than one guide or angel outside of your primary heavenly teammate duo. Even though your team is with you, often many are unaware of their presence. Your team and any soul being in Heaven cannot intervene or assist you in your life without your expressed permission. This is due to that free will law previously mentioned. The law says you will need to request your Spirit team's assistance or guidance. This is also why so many people are led astray down inappropriate or harmful roads. They may not be asking their Spirit team to work with them daily. They also may not believe that there is such a thing or they're ignoring the perpetual warnings from spirit.

For the most part, your Spirit team will assist a

human soul by giving them nudges to head in a direction that will positively benefit them. They will communicate with that soul through their psychic senses and hope the human soul is paying attention. Their job is to help you make sounder choices, but as for anything outside of that, they need your permission. You can give them permission in prayer, affirmations, with your thoughts, out loud, or in writing. You can write them an email and send it to yourself. You call to them and say something like, "I give you permission to intervene with…"

It doesn't matter how you say it, just as long as you let them know. Your soul is built with innate crystal-clear psychic senses for a reason. This is to make your life as comfortable as possible even when you're faced with challenges. The challenges are not as bad as they would be without your strong connection with Heaven. They help you make smarter choices by guiding you through them.

Everyone is born with all psychic clair channels, but typically one or two of the channels are stronger than the others. If you feel that you do not have any clair channels, then that means there are blocks that have closed it up, because everyone has these clairs. No one is more special than anyone else where psychic abilities are concerned. Everyone has varying ways in which they communicate and pick up on Divine assistance.

Someone might have a stronger Clairaudience channel where they hear the voice of spirit, while another person might have a strong sense of knowing the answers. Others feel the guidance coming into them, and then you have the Clairvoyants who receive messages through visual cues. The clairs are always there and accessible to you. They can be opened up when you make healthy positive life changes. When you govern your life through negativity, then this closes the psychic clair channels up. This means that your moods, thoughts, and feelings affect the extra sensory part of you.

When you regularly fall down the path of abusing a toxic challenge, then you will find your clair channels dim to the point that you're unaware of these senses being present at all. Those who run around making negative based comments vocally, or online, have zero connection with anything outside of themselves at that moment. If they do this regularly, then they are indefinitely disconnected from God. A soulless being is someone that does this on a frequent basis. This type of egoist criticism does nothing to help anyone. It doesn't help anyone reading those comments and absorbing the energy surrounding those words. They have no connection to anything outside of the physical. Those connected with Heaven operate from a higher space than those bathed in hate and negativity. This includes spiritually based people, since no one of any group is exempt from hanging out in the areas of negativity, including myself. This is part of the challenges of the physical human life to overcome.

Many are aware that everyone has one main spirit guide and one guardian angel that is with you from the moment you're born in a human body to the moment you depart that human body. If you haven't seen them through Clairvoyance throughout your Earthly life, then when you cross over back home you most definitely will see them in front of you as clear as the day. You will instantly know them like running into a friend you hadn't seen in a while. This realization is immediate and automatic.

When one talks about you having one main spirit guide and guardian angel, what is often left out is how are they with you from human birth and human death? What if someone is a couch potato that sits and watches trash television all day, then gossips on the phone when there is another lull? Is this magnificent Spirit Guide and Guardian Angel hanging around on the couch with that person? I don't know about you, but I'd slit my wrists if I was stuck guiding someone like that. In spiritual reality, I wouldn't feel like a failure that I'm unable to reach that person at all throughout their life, because feelings like failure are non-existent on the Other Side. You just keep trying to get that person's attention repeatedly throughout their life and hope for the best.

The Spirit Guide and Guardian Angel are with the soul in the human body they've soul contractually agreed to be with, stand by, and guide. They are not hanging around the person 24/7 for decades or however long that person lives. The guide and angel have other things they are doing on the Other Side They are alerted to oncoming danger before it takes place because their psychic foresight is at the 100% mark. They know all before anyone does or says anything the same way God does. They can see the projected outcome of this circumstance coming in before it happens. They can then guide the soul away from that danger. There is never an incident where a Spirit Guide or Guardian Angel is late to an incident. It's impossible due to their psychic radar and the incredible access they have to that person's complicating and intricate soul records. They know what's about to take place. If a person is operating with free will, which many tend to do, and they're heading for danger, the guide and angel are alerted way in advance of a probable outcome that's about to happen, so they have plenty of time to warn the person. At that point, they can only hope that the person is tuned in enough to pick up on those warnings.

One of the benefits of being in constant communication with God and your Spirit team is that they become a part of your daily life. When you are talking to them about an issue that's popped up that someone else did that affected you, they are already there and present to help you do something about it so that you can move on from it and onto more important things.

My mother recalled a story when I was eight years old and accompanied her at the local mall. I walked away from her independently as I tend to still do today with everyone it seems. She was looking around to see where I went and found me staring at this shelf filled with angel statues. She said she remembers I had a furious expression on my face. Perplexed while watching me turn towards her angrily shouting while pointing to the statues, "Why are they all blonde with wings?! That's not how they look!"

Ah, the injustice was boiling the inner waters of this warrior soul to a furious rage. That's because the depiction of angels in artwork has forever presented angels in a manner that is inaccurate to what they truly look like, but instead in a way that is more comfortable for people to accept.

One of the other things that would cause a sneer is that guardian angel depictions are usually cutesy cherub little fluffy angels. It's no wonder there are so many skeptics, because no reasonable and rational person could possibly believe they look like cute cuddly stuffed animals. There are cherub looking angels on the Other Side, but they deal more with matters of love, and they are far from cuddly. I'm thinking of the Munchkins in the Wizard of Oz. Ferocious with grand reasonable personalities.

For centuries, there have been countless stories of people encountering an angel in physical form. This is from both believers and non-believers alike. They've been recounted in every holy book in every religion known to man. Regardless of someone's personal belief system, nearly 80% of the planet has a strong belief in angels even if they're not religious. That's every 8 out of 10 people. This is because when they encounter one on those rare occasions there is no doubt. Many that have had angel encounters protested to not believing "in any of that". This changed after the encounter that was deep and profound enough that it altered their conscious perception. Many have experienced similar encounters with an angel especially during traumatic or dire circumstances. Those are the venues where an angel makes its presence known. Angels tend to show up as the person needs it. It's those little reminders that tell you that you are not alone.

Angels show up and hear your prayers and remain present during a time that it's most needed, especially for those with rapidly failing health. When it's someone's time to go back home to Heaven, then the angels and that person's Spirit team along with other beings from Heaven are standing around that person working double time. It's kind of like when an entire family goes to pick someone up at the airport and arrives just before the person has landed. You're standing around waiting for their arrival to pick them up and take them with you. There is often more than one spirit being waiting along with the Archangel Azrael, the angel of death, which is not as cryptic as that sounds. If the person is in the hospital, but has three months to live, then in addition to that persons Spirit team being present throughout, deceased relatives begin flocking within the last number of days as well too.

Angels don't have eyes, as creepy as that might sound to imagine, because we're used to everyone having eyes. They also don't have an anatomy. Even though paintings of angels show them as looking like human beings. In movies they're made to look like us, so everyone thinks or believes they look like a man or a woman.

Angels are a magnificent bright light source created out of God's fire to act as His trusty strong and compassionate assistants. Like all beings, angels can and do morph into the appearance of something human. When they do morph into a human being, their eyes are one of the first initial ways to recognize them, because their eyes, which can be any color, are striking and pierce through you.

When people have had angel encounters, they know without a doubt that it was an angel regardless of how it appeared.

My mother once asked, "Where do you get your great sense of humor? It can't be from any of us."

I said without hesitation, "From the Angels."

Because contrary to some beliefs about Heaven being this cold dark place where judgment occurs, they tend to exude traits of joy, humor, and laughter. When you spend enough time with them, then it will rub off on you as it does with me.

You create your circumstances through your intention. Avoid falling into a victim mentality where you blame everything that goes wrong in your life on other people. Or that you did something to make it happen or must have done something bad in another life to deserve it. No one deserves bad things to happen to them, but you have the gift of standing in your power and taking control of your life. You don't have to do it alone when you have God on your side.

When you pay attention to your Spirit team, then you can pick up on when they are guiding you away from harm, or when they guide you towards helpful circumstances. A common theme of the ego is living in denial of the truth. You deny the messages because it's not what you want to hear. It is displeasing to the human ego. Sometimes the messages intended to assist are guiding someone to do something they're against. This can be a circumstance where you're consistently guided to let go of the possibility of a love relationship with someone you desire. Your Spirit team can see how it will end up ahead and it will not end happily in your favor. Or they see the Soul Mate relationship partner you're contracted to connect with coming in soon. Being with the wrong person may delay the connection from happening.

How many times have you received a nudge to go down one road, but instead you went down another? The result was that something negative or challenging popped up in your life. You later say, "I knew I shouldn't have gone down that road. I sensed something was up, but I ignored that feeling." This is a clue as to how your Spirit team is working with you.

The ways people connect with Heaven are vast and varying from one person to the next. Many of my books include the different ways that can assist someone in being a stronger conduit. This includes a lifestyle and attitude perception change that needs to be adopted. This is from the way you think and feel to what you ingest into your physical body.

When you shift direction and embark on a beautiful personal spiritual journey, then you will find wonderful and amazing new circumstances rise up. Even if this is a feeling and state of mind.

This state of mind is where true bliss resides. There is no end date, time limit, or rush to reach the destination you're hoping to achieve. Take your time with it and follow your gut instincts on what action steps to take.

Some try so hard to make a connection with God not realizing that it's the trying so hard part that pushes the connection away. Most of the time the connection with Heaven happens when you're not trying so hard. When you let go of the control, then it comes. This is what that phrase, "Let go and Let God", means. Learn to know yourself better than anybody. Trust your initial gut reaction to hunches that hit you. When you second-guess the message, you believe you're picking up on, then you move further away from the message or guidance you originally got. If you're receiving a strong hunch that continuously comes to you, then make note of that. The hunch will be something positive that does no harm to anyone, including yourself. Moving your well-being state into that of relaxation, open mindedness, and clarity helps in accessing Spirit easily and as naturally as you pick up the phone to call someone.

CHAPTER TWENTY

The Shift in Global Consciousness

A great deal of this chapter was spearheaded by one of my guides, Saint Nathaniel. We cannot willfully deny that there is a shift in consciousness taking place around the world within each individual soul. It has been this way since the dawn of humankind. It takes centuries for human souls to evolve. When you examine Earth's history, you will note how long it's taken for human beings to evolve. It's been repetitively unnecessarily violent, negative, and filled with hate. This is still going on today in a larger way due to how many people have populated the planet over the centuries. You give as many of them as possible access to a technological device with access to social media and you have a deadly weapon on your hands. While we insist and urge one to display love whenever possible, it cannot be denied that the state of humanity is chaotic. This disorder is what will break the dam that allows a shift in consciousness. This madness has been going on throughout the centuries of Earth's history and progression. As the population of human souls has grown - so has pandemonium.

When you experience constant discomfort internally with amplified emotions, then this may feel to be connected to a shift in consciousness. While this is true to an extent, it is more multifaceted than that for us to place a label on it. Humankind desires labels in order to understand circumstances and people in a broader way. The negative side to labels is when you use it to create separation from one another. Any negative feelings prolonged in you can have a variety of factors attributed to it. These factors and effects are connected to the way humankind has designed Earthly life to be with its structures and rules. While having structure and discipline is important to a degree in order to minimize ego generated chaos, it also creates havoc depending on how restricting you are with others.

Someone experiencing prolonged discomfort internally may have developed this at the hands of other people, their surroundings, the boom and noise of technology, lack of exercise, poor diets, and lifestyle choices. These are some of the potential major contributors towards these turbulent feelings. Forcing one into a corner experiencing these symptoms does and can contribute towards that soul having a shift in consciousness. A great awakening and shift in consciousness happens with a human being when they reach a breaking point at some moment in their life. They come to realize that human life and the toxic negativity that exists globally or within their personal life does not make their soul happy. They begin asking the bigger questions such as, "Why am I here? Why does this place exist? There is nothing but anger, chaos, hate, judgment, unfaithfulness, and so on…"

Someone hurts another and that soul's ego feels scarred as a result. They cannot understand how someone can do something to be cruel to another and feel nothing. Someone that feels nothing and acts out violently towards another is someone without consciousness. Although it seems they have no consciousness, they have one in the deepest core of their soul that sits burning like a pilot light waiting to be ignited. Until then they have an aloof detachment from their soul and everything beyond the physical reality they've created.

We've spoken before about the Mayan Calendar and its effects or non-effects long before December 21, 2012, which was the day believed to be the end of the world. The reason we've never gone any further in depth is because there is nothing to talk about. This was a fad that caught on around the globe and had no bearing on anything legitimate. We said December 21, 2012 will come and go like any other day. The day did come and go with no noticeable shift or ending of Earth. The talk began to build in your year 2012 as you moved closer to 12/21/12. The Mayans did not make any sort of prediction that the end of the world would be on this date and nor was a shift intended to take place at that time. The Mayans ended the Calendar on December 21, 2012 because they were invaded by others outside of their tribe forcing them to abandon the project. We ask of you this, to look deeper into how orchestrated was this at that particular time.

Human ego loves to create hype and drama. With that comes temporary excitement or fear energy that the end is near. The ego also enjoys capitalizing on fear for personal gain. There were movies and books put out about the year 2012 and its significance, as well as for entertainment. If you research history throughout the years, you'll discover that there has always been some measure of apocalyptic scare talk every year. This talk is born out of fear. Fear is connected to the ego.

In some circles they turned this fear energy into something positive such as December 21, 2012 being a day where a global shift would take place and usher the universe into a new era. A new era has occurred periodically over the centuries regardless of the Calendar date. This happens as humankind evolves at a slower rate towards the realization that your soul's life is and should be about love. It is not about pushing others down, bullying, or creating a structure of life that contributes to long-term stress, unhappiness, or early intended human death. Love is what thrives and carries on indefinitely. Love feels good to your soul. It uplifts and adds a euphoric feeling of joy and peace to your life. Love blasts away negativity and heals the soul. It empowers and contributes to helping the soul achieve greater heights of consciousness.

There was a tragedy that hit the news on December 14, 2012 that involved a young man going on a shooting rampage in Connecticut. There was another shooting just days before that at a mall in Oregon. This prompted some to believe that it was somehow related and connected to "doomsday" on December 21, 2012. Those acts were committed by the free will of people that were not mentally balanced and should have been given help, but the guidance provided was ignored. When you're disconnected to your soul and anything outside of the material world, then you grow oblivious to the signs where someone is in desperate need of love or intervention.

The world is currently continuing to shift for the better and has been for some time. This is where the light is equal to the dark, but that did not have anything to do with the year 2012. What has been happening over the course of your 20th Century and beyond is a global shift. In the 2000's, you moved into high noon where the dark energy in human souls became equal to the light. This means that there is an equal amount of good and light in ratio to the darkness and hate in the human being. This is witnessed in the human politics arena where you find people seeking and desiring to interfere and control how another person chooses to live their life. This global shift began to accelerate during the 1900's and onward. As the decades progressed, there were more souls being born to usher in this shift with the goal of raising one's consciousness. Many are becoming more aware of their surroundings and how they behave in their life. They are also living in the heavy density of the Earth's atmosphere and not aware of whom they are deep down beneath the physical reality.

As Earth's history continues, there will be newer generations of souls entering a lifetime in a more evolved manner than the previous generations. This is helped along by the current generations who are evolving and passing it down the bloodline. The 2000's and beyond saw the true beginnings of the rise of the technology age. The positives are this is what can and has contributed positively to the growing consciousness in others. Information is readily accessible and spread much quicker than it ever has. This is all part of the shift in consciousness.

The dark and light in humankind have been in constant battle with one another. It feels extremely heightened to you because there are billions of people that inhabit the planet. The way everyone can communicate is instantaneous, but this adds coldness to the soul and the globe. This coldness does not contribute to a rising of one's consciousness. Connections with one another are short lived while others ruthlessly act out for selfish gain. Humankind is struggling to survive and living under immense stress. This does not contribute to a rising of one's consciousness. This creates an overabundance of unhappy, distant, stressed out human beings trying to survive day to day. Their lives feel empty without any excitement. They reach for time wasters or toxic addictions to keep going. This slowly kills that soul's life force, which does not help in shifting their consciousness. There will need to be a massive uproar, anarchy, and outcry that the way human life is currently designed no longer works. You are becoming hip to the truth that you cannot suffocate the soul.

The shift in consciousness can be seen by the way others live and the positive energy they exude. A deeply spiritual person constantly evolving might soon find work or a purpose that enables them to feel this joy. They feel the joy when tackling the elements in your contract. They will set up life in an area on the planet that isn't congested with angry, cold, stressed persons. When they live in a stuffed area then this recommended human design can make them believe there is a shift in consciousness. The disconnect is severe by the hostility that plagues the planet overall. It is what dominated humanity. When you vacate the trenches of that, then this might offer the illusion that humankind is shifting in consciousness. We do not deny that many souls are evolving each of your days. There is a shift in individual consciousness, but globally this has not been seen in some time. It may be centuries before this is seen on a grander scale. Half the world despises anyone who does not agree with one another or who is of another gender, race, political affiliation, sexual orientation, religion, and so on. These labels you created have no connection to soul reality. You have clues as to where you are at in global consciousness shift on media websites. Read what people type into comment boxes to give you an overall feeling as to where the state of humanity is currently at. If a massive awakening and shift has taken place, then this will reveal itself in the positivity that humankind communicates to each other. This will give you a taste of where you are at with a shifting in consciousness globally.

The true spirit within the physical human body has not evolved and expanded above the soul's ego. The ego part of them will make it known verbally or physically. This acting out is not someone whose consciousness is being raised. It is the ego living in fear of those who refuse to live the way it does. Those creating this harm are waking other souls up from slumber. It is waking them up and into the direction of developing a higher consciousness of love. It is waking them up to realize that how others are being treated is morally wrong and not of God. The human ego has a challenging time with coming to terms in understanding that God created souls to be individuals with their own set of personality traits to master and hone in to the best of your abilities. Souls are prevented from raising its consciousness by not displaying one act aligned with love and compassion.

Shifting your consciousness is having an understanding that you are here for the purpose of love. You are here for your soul's growth. You are here to evolve your soul as either student or teacher, or leader, or follower. You have a detachment to the physical. This means you do not identify with labels to separate *(i.e. race, nationality, man, woman, republican, democrat, gay, straight, spiritual, atheist)*. Nor any other label that limits your soul and places you in a box. You are not your job, the clothes you wear, the house you live in, the car you drive, the family you were born to, the physical appearance you work on to attract or feel good about yourself. These are all fads created by humankind to disillusion you into believing that this is who you are.

Raising your consciousness is coming to terms with this design that has duped humankind into believing you are something if you have or identify with material physical properties. Labels were created by humankind in order to separate souls from one another, but it is not who you are.

Raising your soul consciousness includes moving into the space of love for all. It is accepting that you are a soul in a physical body. You love and appreciate all aspects of you. It is to know that hurting, harming, or hating anyone is to not understand who and what you are in spiritual truth. To be a constant complainer lowers your vibration and prevents you from shifting your consciousness into love.

You will easily become submerged into the physical human life with its ever-changing fads and traditions. This can confuse someone into believing that this is who they are. The shifting in consciousness is being aware of this and not being naïve to believing this to be the soul's reality. It is the only reality you know at that time in your life due to how you were raised. It was taught by the generations passed. When you recall incidents in your life from when you were five, six, or seven years old, it will feel as if you're watching a movie about someone else. If it was a wonderful time, then you feel nostalgic and miss it wanting to re-create it in your later years.

As human souls continue to evolve, they will begin the process of passing a love mantra around to their offspring and so forth. The ones who have failed at this are the ones that have trained their children to hate and cause harm on others different from them. This shift in consciousness will take time since it is a generational shift in consciousness that is happening. This has progressively been going on since the beginning of humankind.

There is a war between the light and dark. Those of the light are the ones with a higher consciousness and the dark being the ones attempting to stop that from happening. This is seen all around the world as humankind attempts to assert itself through the darkness of their ego. If one wants to see how things are changing in a way that benefits this shift in consciousness, then look back through history. How long did it take for women to be treated and considered equal? How long did it take before humankind stopped treating African Americans as slaves? How long was it before someone that identifies as gay was able to marry someone they love? How long did it take before religions accepted other religions? How long did it take for certain circumstances to happen if at all? You can note that some of these situations you've set up have slightly improved, but it took centuries to come about and even still it's not widely accepted by human ego despite what your laws suggest.

These examples are to illustrate what it means to shift your consciousness globally. While it appears, this is beginning to improve and speed up, it will take a while longer to reach that place of peace on Earth. Earth is a ticking time bomb and many human beings are waking up in larger numbers to the idea that the negative way you treat one another is the real sin. Having this awareness is where the true shift in consciousness resides.

When you are not exuding and displaying love, understanding, and compassion, then you do not know God. When you step through the gates of Heaven, it is an overflowing love you experience that never lets up. Love is the reason you are here. Love is the answer to the big questions you have about why you are here and why everything was created. It was for the soul to learn to love and experience love. When you love any soul, only then are you closer to that goal. All circumstances and paths are connected to love and lead to love. Whenever you're in doubt, bring your soul back to this space of love that lives deep within you even if you have forgotten that it ever existed. You were born from love, you entered an Earthly life from love, and you are made up of love. Nothing else matters in the end but love.

Final Words from Author

Heaven is real and I know this because I've seen it through Clairvoyance on more occasions than I can count. I've experienced it and been taken through it. I blink my eyes and the various images and messages of the spirit world flash in front of me without warning and then evaporate. This has been going on for as long as I can remember. From the moment I was born, I had one foot in the physical world and the other foot in the world where I came from. As a four-year-old, I was seeing and hearing spirit in a profound way that I never thought twice about it. Those around me noticed this during the moments I would tell them something that ended up coming to fruition.

When you pass on, then you're left with your soul. All your physical items and worries or concerns are irrelevant with the snap of a finger. If all your left with is your soul's consciousness, then why not give it more attention while you're here. I've relayed descriptions of the Other Side throughout some of my work. From my near-death experience that cracked my portal open and shifted me down a holier path, to the process your soul endures as it crosses over, to the differences between the souls in Heaven with those on Earth, and to the magical paradise of life in Heaven. There is something else beyond this dimension and I've been experiencing it throughout this current life. The glimpses they continue to give me while

I'm here are reminders of what's important and to ignore the cattle and noise of the human ego that will attempt to get in the way. In comparison, the other worlds make life on Earth trivial and more accurately aligned with Hell. Yet, there are glimpses of Heaven in its rarity attempting to shine its way through the thick thud of the aura of the state of the human body by those that are working to raise their vibration and soul consciousness. If only all people would work to keep their vibration high full time. What a peaceful, blissful and loving heavenly world this planet would be!

Soul Consciousness and Purpose

KEVIN HUNTER

Acknowledgments

Thank you to God, my Spirit Team Council, and to all of the loyal readers that have hopped on this awesome train ride of mine and stayed on. I am forever blessed and grateful for your eternal support of the work we do. Thank you also for supporting the arts and the artists of the world.

ALSO BY KEVIN HUNTER

Stay Centered Psychic Warrior
Warrior of Light
Empowering Spirit Wisdom
Darkness of Ego
Realm of the Wise One
Transcending Utopia
Reaching for the Warrior Within
Spirit Guides and Angels
Soul Mates and Twin Flames
Raising Your Vibration
Divine Messages for Humanity
Connecting with the Archangels
Monsters and Angels
The Seven Deadly Sins
Love Party of One
Twin Flame Soul Connections
A Beginner's Guide to the Four Psychic Clair Senses
Tarot Card Meanings
Attracting in Abundance
Abundance Enlightenment
Living for the Weekend
Ignite Your Inner Life Force
Awaken Your Creative Spirit
The Essential Kevin Hunter Collection
Metaphysical Divine Wisdom (Series)

STAY CENTERED PSYCHIC WARRIOR
A Psychic Medium's Trip Through the Darkness and Light of the Spirit Worlds, and Other Paranormal Phenomena

In *Stay Centered Psychic Warrior*, metaphysical teacher, psychic, medium, and author, Kevin Hunter talks about what it's like battling between mental health issues and the deeply potent psychic input that continuously falls into his soul's consciousness throughout each day. He offers plenty of examples and discussions of his brushes with spirit, seeing and hearing the dead, the power of the Darkness and the Light in both the physical and spirit worlds, along with sharing his numerous personal psychic and mediumship essays, glimpses of the Other Side, near death experiences, past lives, soul contracts, traveling to and from the Spirit Worlds spirit guides and angels, recognizing your own psychic gifts, and much more!

This unique autobiography focuses on psychic and mediumship related content coupled with the soul's journey and purpose. Stay Centered Psychic Warrior is an intensely forceful and revealing read that doesn't shy away from the uncomfortable, the Darkness, abuse, mental health issues, while uplifting it with the many blessings of the Light and intriguing day to day psychic phenomena all in one. Allow it to inspire you to recognize your own psychic gifts knowing there is much more to this Earthly life than can be seen or comprehended. Be empowered to break through the rubble and stand strong and centered under the powerful Light that shines through any Darkness.

A Beginner's Guide to the
FOUR PSYCHIC CLAIR SENSES

Many believe psychic gifts are bestowed upon select chosen ones, while others don't believe in the craft at all. The reality is every soul is born with heightened psychic gifts and capabilities, but somewhere along the way those senses have dimmed. All are capable of being a conduit with the other side, including those closed off and blocked to it. There are a variety of enlightened beings residing in the spirit realms to assist human souls that request their help. They use varying means and methods to communicate with you called clair channels. These clairs are crystal clear etheric senses used to communicate with any higher being, spirit guide, angel, departed loved one, archangel, and God.

The *Four Psychic Clair Senses* illustrates what the core senses are, examples of how the author picks up on messages, how you can recognize the guidance, and other fun metaphysical psychic stuff. You are a walking divination tool that allows you to communicate with Spirit. The clairs enable you to receive heavenly messages, guidance, and information that positively assist you or another along your Earthly journey. Read about the four core clairs in order to pinpoint what best describes you and how to have a better understanding of what they are and how they work for you.

TAROT CARD MEANINGS

Tarot Card Meanings is an encyclopedia reference guide that takes the Tarot apprentice reader through each of the 78 Tarot Cards offering the potential general meanings and interpretations that could be applied when conducting a reading. The meanings included can be applied to most anything whether it be spiritual, love, general, or work-related questions.

Many novices struggle with reading the Tarot as they want to know what a card can mean in their readings. They grow stuck staring at three cards side by side and having no idea what it could be telling them. The Tarot Card Meanings book can assist by pointing you in the general direction of where to look. It will not give you the ultimate answers and should not be taken verbatim, as that is up to you as the reader to come to that conclusion. The more you practice, read, and study the Tarot, then the better you become.

Tarot Card Meanings avoids diving into the Tarot history, or card spreads and symbolism, but instead focuses solely on the potential meaning of a card in a general, love, or work reading. This gives you a structure to jump from, but it is up to you to take that energy and add the additional layers to your reading, while trusting your higher self, intuition, instincts and Spirit team's guidance and messages. Anything included in the Tarot Card Meanings book is an overview and not intended to be gospel. It is merely one suggested version of the potential meanings of each of the 78 Tarot cards in a reading. It may assist the novice that is having trouble interpreting cards for themselves.

KEVIN HUNTER

ALSO AVAILABLE BY KEVIN HUNTER

Books that Empower, Enlighten, Educate, and Entertain!

*Just as your body needs physical food to survive,
your soul needs spiritual food for well-being nourishment.*

THE ESSENTIAL KEVIN HUNTER COLLECTION

Kevin Hunter an empowering author specializing in a variety of genres, but he is most notably known for his work in the realms of spirituality, metaphysical, and self-help. He has assisted people around the world with standing in their power, and in having a stronger connection with Heaven, while navigating the materialistic practical world. Now some of his popular spiritually based books are available in this one gigantic volume.

The Essential Kevin Hunter Collection is the spiritual bible that contains over 500 pages of content geared towards improving and enhancing your life. It is for those who prefer everything in one gigantic book. The content included in this edition are from the books: *Spirit Guides and Angels, Soul Mates and Twin Flames, Raising Your Vibration, Divine Messages for Humanity, Connecting with the Archangels, Warrior of Light, Empowering Spirit Wisdom,* and *Darkness of Ego.*

TRANSCENDING UTOPIA
Reopening the Pathway to Divinity

Transcending Utopia is packed with practical and spirit knowledge that focuses on enhancing your life through empowering divinely guided spiritual related teachings, inspiration, wisdom, guidance, and messages. The way to accelerate existence on Earth towards Utopia is if every person on the planet resided in their soul's true nature, which is in a state of all love, joy, and peace. The ultimate Nirvana is surpassing that perfection through methods that a limited consciousness could ever dream possible. This is the exceptional glory your soul was born into before the dense turbulence of Earthly life enveloped and suffocated you.

Transcending Utopia is to go beyond your limits and travel outside of the generic mundane materialistic achievement that human beings taught one another to thrive for. A utopian society is where everything is perfectly blissful on all levels according to the sanctified values you were born with. The sensations connected to how flawless everything feels in that moment reveals the authentic perfection you were made from. Utopia is the ideal paradise as imagined in one's dreams that seems to be inaccessible by human standards. It is a state of mind that is possible to reach by adopting broader ways of looking at circumstances while being disciplined about how you conduct your life. You search for a sign of this utopia through external means, only to be consistently left with disappointment. This is because utopia begins and ends inside the spark that burns within your spirit like a pilot light waiting to be ignited.

LIVING FOR THE WEEKEND
*The Winding Road Towards Balancing
Career Work and Spiritual Life*

Working hard to ensure your bills are paid can leave your soul spiritually starved for soul nourishment. When your goal is to obtain enough money to be comfortable that you become carried away in that current, then there is little to no room for Divine enrichment.

Many work to survive in jobs they hate because it's the way it is. As a result, they experience and endure all sorts of emotional pain whether it is through depression, sadness, anger, or any other kind of negative stressor. Some silently suffer through this emotional strain gradually killing off their life force. If you don't have a healthy social life and positive fun filled activities and hobbies to balance that burden outside of that, then that could add additional tension. What's it all for if you can't live the life you've always wanted to live? Instead, you spend your days growing forever miserable and broken.

Living for the Weekend examines the pitfalls, struggles, as well as the benefits available in the current modern-day working world. This is followed up with spiritual and practical tips, guidance, messages, and discussions on ways to incorporate more balance and enlightenment to a cutthroat material driven world.

Attracting in Abundance
Opening the Divine Gates to Inviting in Blessings and Prosperity Through Body, Mind, and Soul Spirit

Having enough money to survive comfortably enough on this physical plane is part of obtaining abundance, but it's not the destination and purpose to thrive for. You could work hard to make enough money to the point you are set for life, but that won't necessarily equate to happiness. Achieving a content satisfied state of joy and serenity starts with examining your soul's state and overall well-being. When that's in place, then the rest will follow.

Attracting in Abundance combines practical and spirit wisdom surrounding the nature of abundance. This is something that most everyone can get on board with because all human beings desire physical comforts, blessings, and prosperity, regardless of their personal values and belief systems. *Attracting in Abundance* is broken up into three parts to help move you towards inviting abundance into your life on all levels. "Part One" contains some no-nonsense lectures surrounding the philosophies, concepts, and debates on the laws of attracting in abundance. "Part Two" is the largest of the sections geared towards fine tuning the soul into preparing for abundance. "Part Three" is the final lesson plan to help crack open the gates of abundance with various helpful tidbits, guidance, and messages as well as the blocks that can prevent abundance from coming in.

The B-Side to the Attracting in Abundance book

ABUNDANCE ENLIGHTENMENT
*An Easy Motivational Guide to
the Laws of Attracting in Abundance
and Transforming Your Soul*

Ultimate authentic success surrounds your soul's growth and evolving process. It's when you realize that none of the physical ego driven desires matter in the end. You can work hard to make sure you stay afloat, you're able to pay your bills, and support yourself and family, but you're not chasing popularity for external validation. Any amount of goodness displayed from your heart is the true measure of real accomplishment.

An overflowing feeling of optimism and love coupled with faith and action is what increases the chances of attracting good things and positive experiences to you. Abundance is more than monetary and financial increase. It can also be about reaching an optimistic well-being state of joy, peace, and love. This positive emotional mindful state simultaneously attracts in blessings.

Abundance Enlightenment is the follow up book to *Attracting in Abundance*. It contains both practical guidance and spirit wisdom that can be applied to everyday life. Some of the key topics surround the laws of attraction as well as healthier money management and improving your soul to help make you a fine tuned in abundance attractor.

MONSTERS AND ANGELS
An Empath's Guide to Finding Peace in a Technologically Driven World Ripe with Toxic Monsters and Energy Draining Vampires

Every person on the planet is capable of being empathic and sensitive, to becoming an energy vampire or toxic monster. No one is exempt from displaying the darker sides of their ego. The easiest and most efficient way to spread any kind of energy is online. Every time you log onto the Internet, there is a larger chance you're going to see something related to the news, media, or gossip areas thrown in front of you, even if you attempt to avoid it as much as possible. You're absorbing everything that your consciousness faces, including the ugly and the wicked, which has its own consequences. This tempestuous energy is tossed into the Universe ultimately creating a flame-throwing battleground inside and around you.

Monsters and Angels discusses how technology, media, and social media have an immense power in distributing both positive and negative influences far and wide. This is about being mindful of what can negatively affect your state of being, and how to counter and avoid that when and wherever possible. Therefore, it's beneficial to govern yourself, your life, and your surroundings like a strict disciplined executive.

TWIN FLAME SOUL CONNECTIONS
Recognizing the Split Apart, the Truths and Myths of Twin Flames, Soul Love Connections, Soul Mates, and Karmic Relationships

Twin Flames have a shared ongoing sentiment and quest from the moment they're a spark shooting out of God's love that explodes into a blinding white fire that breaks apart causing one to be two, until two become one again, separate and whole, and back around again. Looking into the eyes of your Twin Flame is like looking into the eyes of God, because to know love is to know God.

Twin Flame Soul Connections discusses and lists some of the various myths and truths surrounding the Twin Flames, and how to identify if you've come into contact with your Twin Flame, or if you know someone who has. The goal is not to find ones Twin Flame, but to awaken one's heart to love, and to work on becoming complete and whole as an individual soul through spiritual self-mastery, life lessons, growth, and raising your consciousness. Your soul's life was born out of love and will die right back into that love.

WARRIOR OF LIGHT
Messages from my Guides and Angels

There are legions of angels, spirit guides, and departed loved ones in heaven that watch and guide you on your journey here on Earth. They are around to make your life easier and less stressful. Learn how you can recognize the guidance of your own Spirit team of guides and angels around you. Author, Kevin Hunter, relays heavenly guided messages about getting humanity, the world, and yourself into shape. He delivers the guidance passed onto him by his own Spirit team on how to fine tune your body, soul and raise your vibration. Doing this can help you gain hope and faith in your own life in order to start attracting in more abundance.

EMPOWERING SPIRIT WISDOM
A Warrior of Light's Guide on Love, Career and the Spirit World

Kevin Hunter relays heavenly, guided messages for everyday life concerns with his book, *Empowering Spirit Wisdom*. Some of the topics covered are your soul, spirit and the power of the light, laws of attraction, finding meaningful work, transforming your professional and personal life, navigating through the various stages of dating and love relationships, as well as other practical affirmations and messages from the Archangels. Kevin Hunter passes on the sensible wisdom given to him by his own Spirit team in this inspirational book.

DARKNESS OF EGO

In *Darkness of Ego*, author Kevin Hunter infuses some of the guidance, messages, and wisdom he's received from his Spirit team surrounding all things ego related. The ego is one of the most damaging culprits in human life. Therefore, it is essential to understand the nature of the beast in order to navigate gracefully out of it when it spins out of control. Some of the topics covered in *Darkness of Ego* are humanity's destruction, mass hysteria, karmic debt, and the power of the mind, heaven's gate, the ego's war on love and relationships, and much more.

REACHING FOR THE WARRIOR WITHIN

Reaching for the Warrior Within is the author's personal story recounting a volatile childhood. This led him to a path of addictions, anxiety and overindulgence in alcohol, drugs, cigarettes and destructive relationships. As a survival mechanism, he split into many different "selves." He credits turning his life around, not by therapy, but by simultaneously paying attention to the messages he has been receiving from his Spirit team in Heaven since birth.

REALM OF THE WISE ONE

In the Spirit Worlds and the dimensions that exist, reside numerous kingdoms that house a plethora of Spirits that inhabit various forms. One of these tribes is called the Wise Ones, a darker breed in the spirit realm who often chooses to incarnate into a human body one lifetime after another for important purposes.

The *Realm of the Wise One* takes you on a magical journey to the spirit world where the Wise Ones dwell. This is followed with in-depth and detailed information on how to recognize a human soul who has incarnated from the Wise One Realm. Author, Kevin Hunter, is a Wise One who uses the knowledge passed onto him by his Spirit team of Guides and Angels to relay the wisdom surrounding all things Wise One. He discusses the traits, purposes, gifts, roles, and personalities among other things that make up someone who is a Wise One. Wise Ones have come in the guises of teachers, shaman, leaders, hunters, mediums, entertainers and others. *Realm of the Wise One* is an informational guide devoted to the tribe of the Wise Ones, both in human form and on the other side.

IGNITE YOUR INNER LIFE FORCE

Ignite Your Inner Life Force is an introduction guide for teens, young adults, and anyone seeking answers, messages, and guidance and surrounding spiritual empowerment. This is from understanding what Heaven, the soul, and spiritual beings are to knowing when you are connecting with your Spirit team of Guides and Angels. Some of the topics covered are communicating with Heaven, working with your Spirit team, what your higher self is, your life purpose and soul contract, what the ego is, love and relationships, your vibration energy, shifting your consciousness and thinking for yourself even when you stand alone. This is an in-depth primer manual offering you foundation as you find a higher purpose navigating through your personal journey in today's modern-day practical world.

AWAKEN YOUR CREATIVE SPIRIT

Your creative spirit is more than being artistic and getting involved in creativity pursuits, although this is a good part of it. When your creative spirit is activated by a high vibration state of being, then this is the space you create from. You can apply this to your dealings in life, your creative and artistic pursuits, and to having a greater communication line with your Spirit team on the Other Side. *Awaken Your Creative Spirit* is an overview of what it means to have access to Divine assistance and how that plays a part in arousing the muse within you in order to bring your state of mind into a happier space.

KEVIN HUNTER

THE *WARRIOR OF LIGHT* SERIES OF POCKET BOOKS

Spirit Guides and Angels, Soul Mates and Twin Flames, Raising Your Vibration, Connecting with the Archangels, Twin Flame Soul Connections, Attracting in Abundance, Monsters and Angels, The Four Psychic Clair Senses, The Seven Deadly Sins, Love Party of One, Abundance Enlightenment, and *Divine Messages for Humanity*

METAPHYSICAL DIVINE WISDOM
BOOK SERIES

On Psychic Spirit Team Heaven Communication
On Soul Consciousness and Purpose
On Increasing Prayer with Faith for an Abundant Life
On Balancing the Mind, Body, and Soul
On Manifesting Fearless Assertive Confidence
On Universal, Physical, Spiritual and Soul Love

♥

About Kevin Hunter

Kevin Hunter is the metaphysical author of dozens of spiritually based books that include *Warrior of Light, Transcending Utopia, Stay Centered Psychic Warrior, Metaphysical Divine Wisdom Series, Empowering Spirit Wisdom, Realm of the Wise One, Reaching for the Warrior Within, Darkness of Ego, Living for the Weekend, Ignite Your Inner Life Force, Awaken Your Creative Spirit,* and *Tarot Card Meanings*.

His pocket books include, *Spirit Guides and Angels, Soul Mates and Twin Flames, Raising Your Vibration, Divine Messages for Humanity, Connecting with the Archangels, The Seven Deadly Sins, Four Psychic Clair Senses, Monsters and Angels, Twin Flame Soul Connections, Attracting in Abundance, Love Party of One* and *Abundance Enlightenment*. His non-spiritual related works include the horror drama, *Paint the Silence*, and the modern-day love story, *Jagger's Revolution*.

Kevin started out in the entertainment business in 1996 as the personal development assistant guy to one of Hollywood's most respected acting talents, Michelle Pfeiffer, at her former boutique production company, Via Rosa Productions. She dissolved her company after several years and he made a move into coordinating film productions for the studios. His film credits include One Fine Day, A Thousand Acres, The Deep End of the Ocean, Crazy in Alabama, The Perfect Storm, Original Sin, Harry Potter & the Sorcerer's Stone, Dr. Dolittle 2, and Carolina. He considers himself a beach bum born and raised in Southern California. For more information and books visit: www.kevin-hunter.com

www.ingramcontent.com/pod-product-compliance
Lightning Source LLC
Chambersburg PA
CBHW061428040426
42450CB00007B/943